WANNA-BE'S

Mark Connelly

Acknowledgments

"Insignificant Others" appeared in *The Great American Literary Magazine*, Issue 1. Fall 2014.

COVER PHOTO CREDITS
Copyright: <a href='http://www.123rf.com/profile_peshkova'>peshkova / 123RF Stock Photo</a>

TABLE OF CONTENTS

Insignificant Others	3
The Color of Liberation	9
Gimme Shelter	31
"Can We Talk?"	49
The Prize	57
Hip-Hop	73
Ghost of the Ruptured Duck	81
A Sip of Amontillado	103
Chalk Men	115
Wiseguys	127
Luck of the Irish	147
Point of Order	161
Thy Name is Woman	179

INSIGNIFICANT OTHERS

Winfield Payton awoke to a mother's voice. Not his mother—but someone's mother. It was the commanding yet compassionate voice mothers develop, stern but apprehensive. It was a voice rarely heard in Downer Estates, a brick apartment complex housing the usual collection of upscale "singles" who live within Frisbee range of urban universities, attend jazz concerts in the park, practice safe sex, drive alphabet cars (BMWs, SUVs, VWs), cybersex on company laptops, faithfully recycle Perrier bottles, and sip low-cal cappuccino in Starbucks while checking the fates of their mutual funds.

It was a suburban voice, a beach voice, a picnic voice. The voice of a concerned mother directing her brood. "Now, look, Brandy, I told you before. Mommy will be home in just a little while. You can have cereal. Where is Heather? OK, tell Heather to give you some raisin bran. Take your vitamin. And don't go near the pool until I get back. Do you understand? Don't go swimming until Mommy comes home."

As yet Win had not opened his eyes; he was too exhausted. Confronting daylight would be painful. Feeling the sun warm his naked back, he buried his face in the pillows. For a moment he imagined he was at Bradford Beach, snoozing while mommies and kiddies trooped over him, sprinkling his blanket with sand and popsicle drippings.

But no, he was in bed. His bed. His fingers felt the familiar smooth lacquered headboard. The pillow bore the scent of Old Spice, his cologne—mundane but reliable.

Home. He turned his aching neck. This simple movement triggered intracranial alarms. Now everything hurt. His head throbbed. His neck tightened. His back ached. Streaks of raw flesh burned across his chest and thighs.

Oh! His body bore the imprint of what his clouded mind failed to recall. Opening an eye to the sun, he saw a gleaming bottle of Absolut on the bedside table. The bottle was nearly empty. Oh! A ceramic ashtray held the twisted remains of weedy joints. Oh! Two broken poppers lay on the carpet. Oh! Leaning over, he saw—amid the tangled debris of his clothes—three lipstick-stained balls of Kleenex, each containing a spent condom. Oh!

Rolling over, Win groaned, feeling like a crash victim. The female voice in the other room called out to him. No longer the mommy voice, it was the supportive, deferential, eager-to-please voice of a Sixties sitcom wife. Mary Tyler Moore exuding "Oh, Rob!" compassion. "Do you want Motrin?" she asked, "I'm making coffee." He heard the sounds of housewife bustling in his bachelor kitchen.

"Motrin," he croaked, like a wounded GI begging for morphine. Motrin, hell. He needed intensive care. IV's. Oxygen. And Band-Aids. Sitting up, blinking in the sunlight, Win noted the thin, blood-lined scratches and nicks across his chest and thighs. Steve McQueen tangled by barbed wire in *The Great Escape*.

"Here, baby."

The woman standing in the doorway bore no relation to the voice flowing with flight attendant charm. Despite the black eye makeup, false eyelashes, and hooker-red lipstick, she was clearly pretty. Her sensibly short blonde hair was cutely, boyishly cut. It complemented the husband-bought Mother's Day earrings. No doubt she had been trying to look like Debra Harry since fifth grade.

Below the chin she was decidedly dissimilar. Her neck was gripped by a two-inch leather choker studded with steel points. Metal chains led to a leather corset which maximized her cleavage and girdled her waist with tight belts and more chains. Handcuffs dangled over a thigh encased in torn fishnet. Her wrists and ankles sported matching leather cuffs.

Instinctively, Win drew back. Only her soft voice reminded him that he was not in mortal danger.

"Oh, baby, look at those scratches. I'm so sorry! I forget about these nails." She wiggled the fingers of her right hand, their dagger-like points flashing blood-red in the sunlight. Her left palm cupped three red caplets.

He took the pills, then, reaching for a water glass accidentally gulped three and half ounces of Absolut. God!

"Oh, honey!"

Sitting up, Win rubbed his eyes and brushed his unruly hair. The woman sat on the edge of the bed and began unbuckling her cuffs, dropping them into a black leather shoulder bag.

"Mind if I take a quick shower? I have to get home to the kids."

"Go ahead, Barbie." Barbie. Gratefully her name came back to him. She disappeared into the guest bath. The architects of Downer Estates had thoughtfully equipped each two-bedroom apartment with two full baths. Single tenants and their partners of choice could shower at the same time, going through their customary after-sex hygienic rituals in private. Alone in the main bath, Win gargled with

Scope, doused his sore member with hydrogen peroxide, then drew a bath.

Sitting in the steaming water, he felt his muscles unwind. Since his thirty-seventh birthday, a loosening morning bath had become a necessity before he could take a shower and actually wash. Rubbing his neck, Win heard water running in the next room. The grip of alcohol fading, the night's events played over in his mind.

Win had naively assumed that one had to call an escort service, troll BDSM dating sites, or stalk FetLife profiles to locate someone like Barbie Monreal. It seemed highly unlikely to run into a woman with her tastes at a real estate seminar.

Normally, Win avoided attractive professional women with wedding rings—unless he met them in a singles bar. A real estate seminar held in the student union of his own college was an improbable place to get lucky. Money rather than lust was on his mind that afternoon. He accepted Barbie's Century 21 card gracefully enough and was prepared to move onto the next booth when she suggested a rendezvous at Henri's for drinks.

Barbie Monreal reminded him of Doris Day in *Please Don't Eat the Daisies*. Attractive. Cute. But too domesticated to arouse any libidinous interests—until her third white wine spritzer, when, suitably lubricated, she calmly announced her motives.

"Now that the kids are older, and I have some time, I'd like to get back into psychodrama."

"Acting?" Win asked naively.

"In a way," she smiled, giving him a patronizing nod. "Role play. Fantasy. I like the tension, the intimacy. I like power. Both asserting and receiving. Strength and submission. It's like sexual I Ching. Give. Take. Dominate. Submit. But nothing violent, you understand. I play it safe, sane, and consensual," she said as if repeating radio jingle. "Nothing too perverse."

"Nothing too perverse?"

"Consider it a hard massage. I like it both ways, but nothing painful."

"Nothing painful," Win repeated, recalling his dentist's reassuring lie about the ease of root canal.

"Not at all. I mostly like the costumes. It's like adult Halloween."

"Halloween?"

"Sure. Like playing dress up. Gives you a chance to let your mind go, explore the dark side. It's the ultimate safe sex. You can't even consider it cheating. Not really. I never do straight. Well, maybe oral," she added quietly, sounding like a dieter surrendering to a Weight Watcher sundae.

"I have the rest of the afternoon off," she said, fixing her eyes on him with Nancy Reagan admiration.

Thus began the first of many encounters, most of which Win could only perform or endure under the influence of alcohol.

Lying in the tub, Win rubbed his temples, then forced himself out of the warm embryonic water to shower and, more tentatively, shave.

Clad in a bathrobe, Barbie was making his bed when he returned. She fluffed the pillows, smoothed the comforter, then collected the accouterments of modern romance— body oil, vibrator, adult DVDs, and five-inch spike heels.

"Honey, you really shouldn't drink so much." She smiled, offering him coffee.

He nodded, taking burning gulps of Eight O'Clock French Roast.

As Winfield dressed, he watched Barbie slip into white pantyhose, cream skirt, white blouse, sensible heels, and gold Century 21 blazer.

"I've got to buzz home to check on the kids," she said, consulting her smart phone. "I've got appointments the rest of the day. Do you want to get together Thursday? Around two?"

"Sure," Win agreed, feeling like a casual user sliding into addiction.

The July morning was cool. He walked Barbie to her car. "You know, I lived in New York right after college," she said. "West Seventy-Second. I love that town. Went to Hellfire once. Didn't like it." She wrinkled her nose as if recalling a disappointing dessert at Le Cirque.

Still the neophyte, Win volunteered an apology, "I hope I didn't hurt your wrist."

"Oh, this?" She pulled back her sleeve, revealing a circle of darkened flesh. "My bruises fade. I tell Jerry they come from aerobics."

They reached her car, a dark blue Volvo bearing a "Have You Hugged Your Kids Today?" bumper sticker. She opened the trunk and dropped in the black shoulder bag with a heavy thud.

Donning sunglasses, she smiled at Win. "Until Thursday. If something comes up, text me."

Win nodded, the fresh air reviving his headache.

"Look, Win, I've just gotten to know you. I realize I shouldn't make any judgments or tell you how to live your life, but I am beginning to care about you. As a special friend." She paused, grating the steel tip of her heel against the curb. "Win, I think you should seriously consider going condo."

THE COLOR OF LIBERATION

"And the best thing about it, Win—you look black." Turning from the controls of the Lear jet, Brooks Adams adjusted his Foster Grants and broke an Eddie Murphy grin, "I mean on paper. Think about it! *Win-field Pay-ton*. That could be a black guy's name, right?"

"Thank God my parents didn't name me Sean," Winfield said, self-consciously brushing his blond hair. Win had come to regard his Eurocentric complexion as a handicap for an instructor in an urban community college. He was, his Hispanic dean ceaselessly reminded him, the lone white male English instructor hired in a decade.

"You see," Brooks explained, "some people on the board gave me heat last summer when I brought on Carlos and Bijan. They see a foreign-looking name on our letterhead and go ballistic. They want to know why I didn't hire a brother—meaning, of course, their deadbeat brother-in-law. But I'm running a savings and loan, not a charity. We're not some community based non-profit that can run to the mayor every time we can't pay the light bill. If folks want jobs, they have to bring something to the table.

"The board doesn't understand that a black business can't afford to be insulated. I try telling them that if we don't maintain a little diversity of our own, we risk isolating ourselves. But they're old school. Ministers. Funeral directors. You know that kind of black folk. Conservative. Old-fashioned. Their vision is limited. They want us to be some kind of colored George Bailey Building and Loan outfit. Help a Negro buy a ranch house. Right out of *Raisin in the Sun.* It's a noble idea, but it ain't 1960 anymore. We have to move on. Remember the old days? When all we did were tavern loans and duplex mortgages?"

Winfield nodded. He had first tasted the fruits of capitalism in the damp basement of Frederick Douglass Savings and Loan, helping his college roommate xerox car loan flyers. Brooks' father, a retired Air Force colonel, had staked his pension on a storefront S&L. Cash poor in the summer of '99, he paid his sons and Win in repoed cars. For his services, Winfield was rewarded with a distressed Dodge Dynasty with bullet holes and bad tires. But the effort to bring a Clintonian form of Reaganomics to the inner city paid off, and four years later, Frederick Douglass Savings and Loan moved into a 1910 neo-classic temple that once housed Badger Life and Annuity.

"We have to branch out," Brooks insisted, tapping the controls. "Half the minority loans these days are going to Asians and Hispanics. But if I put out an ad in Spanish, folks on the board jump all over me. They want to keep the S&L a 'black thang.' Talk about growth, the Internet, networking, the global economy, and their eyes glaze over. I wanted to put two hundred thousand into a hotel complex in Scotland. A sure safe sixteen-percent return! But the board went wild. Why should black money go to Scotland? Why don't we buy up some houses in the ghetto and fix them up for poor people? I try to explain the profit motive, and they look at me like I'm selling them the road to Hell.

"That's why I started Frederick Douglass Investments. FDI will have its own board. I got the S&L directors to give us seed capital. OK, we have to report to them, but they won't have to sign off on every deal we make. Anything under a half a mil is beyond their reach. We have to put it in the quarterly report, but we won't have to do a song and dance every time we want to move some money offshore. But they still have to approve key personnel. I managed to squeak Carlos and Bijan through. Well, Winfield C. Payton, Ph.D. won't sound any alarms."

"Tell them I went to Dillard," Winfield said, recalling a distant New Orleans July in the pre-Katrina era. Jungle humidity, four showers a day, wash suits, and lots of chicory coffee and Motrin to face two hours of summer school and ten hours of drinking. And now Bourbon Street was less than thirty minutes away. Nostalgia tugged at him. Boozy, bosomy memories of dancers named Brandy, Star, and Ginger came to mind. Alas, now they would all be past their prime, no doubt living on alimonies or running hair salons in Metairie or Gretna. Winfield was far too discreet, too mature to hang out in topless bars at home, but in the Big Easy visiting a strip joint was almost mandatory, like dropping a roll of quarters into a Vegas slot machine. Maybe, if things went well, they could celebrate at the Sho-Bar before heading home.

"Take this business," Brooks continued. "I gave up trying to explain it to the board. It's simple and profitable. Larry and I fly in the Reserves. So we set up a company delivering aircraft sold at government auctions. We service and deliver. It's all cash, and we get in plenty of flight hours. This baby," he said patting the instrument panel, "was seized by the IRS. Cat in New Orleans bought it. Normally, we fly the bird in and have to deadhead home. But today we have a plane to take to Chicago. So I can afford to bring everyone down to make the presentation.

Show off the whole team. That's why I want you to join FDI officially. I can't pay much. A thousand a month plus an office.

"When the real estate firm on the second floor pulled out, I saw our chance to grow. Instead of renting out the space, I decided to put together a network of entrepreneurs, people who already have steady jobs and benefits. Why hire one executive full-time, when I can pick up four or five people—attorneys, PhD's, all with solid credentials. People who already have a stable base with a pension and benefits but want more, want to do something on their own. People who aren't satisfied with the usual tradeoff. Why should you have to compromise these days? Keisha's got a safe job in her Dad's law firm but wants to take a stab at investments without risking her trust fund. Like you, Bijan works out of a two-by-four faculty cubicle. He can't meet clients there, even if his dean is impressed with the good will and free publicity his consulting gives the department. I see all of us working together. You work part-time for FDI and do your own thing on the side and share what you bring you in. It's a win-win situation. Plus, we can feed each other clients. You can run a public relations agency out of the office. All I ask is a one-third split up to ten thousand a month to cover expenses. Less your thousand. You get that every month, whether you make money on your own or not. Just help out when I want you to and be a phone call away when we need all hands on deck for something special. So what do you think of becoming Dr. Winfield Payton, Communications Director? How's that sound?"

"Sounds like home." Looking at the clouds, Winfield smiled. A thousand a month. An extra six-fifty after taxes would just about cover his credit card payments, which ballooned to national debt proportions each summer.

"I thought MITI was home."

"Sure. A hundred and thirty-five a year plus benefits, but there it stops. I can stay there until death and only see a three to five percent annual growth. I need something more." Pushing forty, Winfield had grown dissatisfied with teaching. It was a lifetime job with as much security as a slot on the Supreme Court, but he felt pinched by its limitations. College pals and ex-girlfriends had made fortunes in real estate and junk bonds, building second and third homes in Phoenix and Key West. Brooks, too, was getting impatient. The big 4-0 was on the horizon, and his chances of being a black Donald Trump or ebony Ted Turner were running out. He lived on the edge, hungering for national recognition. Nothing delighted him more than a Fed-Ex from San Diego or an email from Kuwait.

"Too bad the screenplay didn't turn out," Brooks mused.

"Yes," Winfield sighed, regretting the thousands he'd spent on reading fees for *AM/FM*. Sadly the script reviewers in Japanese-owned studios were uniformly unimpressed by his taut drama about a fired shock jock turned homeless advocate. Someone who knew someone who knew Nipsey Russell's nephew had managed to get it read by an independent producer who promised to discuss Win's project with his partners. But Winfield's chance at making the Hollywood D-list had evidently fizzled out over a three martini lunch in the no smoking section of an outdoor Valley restaurant. His script was returned, crumpled, stained, and burned—evidently having served as an illicit ashtray. And it would have been the perfect resurrection vehicle for Pauly Shore.

"Well, keep plugging. You'll make it yet. Meanwhile there's no reason why you can't make a little money. You always wanted to be Jack Kerouac in a clean shirt."

"This sure beats flying standby," Winfield said, eager to change the topic. He shifted in the contoured seat, his arms still aching from last night's session with Barbie. A stressful closing and a tense PTA meeting had made her especially submissive.

"Enjoy it, the flight back won't be so snug. We're taking back a DC-3 cargo ship. No bar on that bird and no seats—that's why I brought along blankets and sleeping bags."

"Still beats flying commercial."

"Frankly, I couldn't afford to fly the full team anywhere. We've taken on a lot of new expenses. But we have to spend to grow. Bringing on new folks ought to improve our cash flow."

"Well, I opened a savings account and bought a Douglass CD."

Brooks smiled. "Don't forget a car loan, a mortgage, and hell, buy a tavern through us as well. Seriously, adding people expands our network. Bijan has solid ties with the Iranian exile community. His grandfather was a minister in the Shah's government. His family is worth ten to twenty million, and their relatives in California can give us some solid leads on investors. Carlos is tight with the Miami Cubans. And your Dad's outfit—Fitzgerald, Payton, and Ryan . . ."

"Can tap us right into the EU if we need to. . ."

"Hey, does your Dad still have Emerald Isle Investments?"

"You mean Erin-Go-Broke? Sure, it's only part of my grandfather's empire that survived the Crash. Pays about half a percent. Generates ten or twenty grand in commissions a year." Though of dubious investment value, the green gilt-edged certificates, embossed with Gaelic script and festooned with castles and shamrocks, made wonderful St. Patrick's Day gifts.

"Play the Irish card whenever you can. You have to max your opportunities where you find them. Hell, as a Republican, I ought to bash Affirmative Action—but who can turn it down? Tell me if you would? The problem is you have to know how to use it. All those minority quotas just open the door. They let you in to compete, but you have to bring something new to the mix to become a player. That's what most black outfits don't understand. They think all we have to do is show up and do the job just as well as everyone else, maybe a little better to prove ourselves. Well, hell, take away Affirmative Action, and white folks could do that for themselves. We have to provide seven figure names Goldman Sachs never heard of, fresh markets, new prospects, links to investors, and deals they can't touch. Then we become a real asset, not just a social obligation.

"And there is another reason I want you on board. You get along with Lionel, not everyone does. Black folks can be a little intolerant about him. He embarrasses me sometimes, but he's my kid brother. Everyone else, except Keisha, is afraid it will rub off on them. Plus, having a white face in the room keeps us focused. Shel Wertheim says he always wants a goy at the table to keep his people honest. See, it's too easy for minorities to get paranoid, develop the 'us against them' mindset. Everybody's got a horror story to tell, and pretty soon you limit your options and start assuming every white's a bigot. All it takes to diffuse that is one guy in the room to be the token, the exception. I've been there. Been the only niggah in the room and watched people bite their tongues. God knows what they said about spooks when I left to take a leak."

"I'll do my whitest."

"More than that, we need a chiclet—a white guy—to be our public face from time to time. The moment I walk in the door, and people see we're a black outfit, they have us pegged. For good or ill, we get pigeonholed and never get the full story. See, bigots don't bother me. I can spot them in a heartbeat. They don't waste your time. They won't do business with you, no matter what, and you can feel it. It's the whi-whi's—the white whiners—the liberals who give me grief. They're suspicious of black capitalists. We're supposed to be victims, poor oppressed people who only rise through their benevolence. Rich niggers who know the stock market give them the shakes. You could get past that. White folks will be honest with you. See, if I walk in and do a presentation, white folks pitch me softball questions, so I won't feel offended. I leave the room, and they throw the book at a white guy, and he gets the contract because they got a chance to sound him out. I get smiles and a second latté, but he gets vetted. We need a white face, someone to be suitably invisible. You can blend in and test the waters for us. That way our presentations get a full review.

"And you're one of the few white guys I can trust. See, you're used to working with us. You won't get offended if someone vents and says something racist. Black folks need to blow off steam once in a while. You won't hit the ceiling when one of us gets frustrated and rants about the fays.

"And we're going to need your help to pull off Brewer's Court. It's going to be our chance to be major players." He pointed to the brochure on Winfield's lap. "The text you came up is first rate."

"Thanks," Winfield nodded. He had devoted late nights to writing and rewriting glowing descriptions of the proposed renovation of a nineteenth-century brewery. Soon, if enough investors could be attracted, the old brick malt silos and Gothic stone bottling plant would house upscale condos, offices, and exclusive retail outlets. The mayor mentioned the project in his re-election campaign. Investors in New York and San Francisco had expressed interest. Winfield had decided to invest twenty or thirty thousand and, with Barbie's urging, hoped to purchase a condo.

"Frederick Douglass stands a chance to go national with this project. If we can finance twenty percent of it—hell, I want to do at least thirty-five—we'll have credibility on the Coasts. It means working with US Bank, Chase, Northwestern. There will be major investors, pension managers from Illinois and Texas. We build solid relations with the major teachers' retirement funds, and we're in like Flynn. Nothing like a few black faces on their websites to make a pension board look socially responsible."

"Where does Singh Veraswami fit in?"

"I caught him on Tony Brown a few years ago. He teaches at Tulane, but he's coming to Marquette for a year. If we can bring him on board, even in an advisory role, it will get us international attention. Plus, he has some key contacts in Africa. He knows people who want to invest in the American market. That would make us unique, blending African-American and African investments in urban redevelopment. I've talked to Veraswami, and he's interested. He sees what we are trying to do; he understands what I'm trying to explain to our board. Going global to work local. Have you read his book?"

"Some of it," Winfield said, feeling like a fifth grader hit with a pop quiz. He had, in fact, only skimmed the dust jacket and scanned the preface. From the self-congratulatory bio on the fly leaf of *Liberation Capitalism*, Winfield gleaned that Dr. Singh Veraswami saw himself as a combination Malcolm X and Dale Carnegie, extolling black empowerment through the magic of compound interest and leverage buyouts.

Winfield pulled a copy from his briefcase. Leafing through the pages, as if seeking a favorite passage, he asked, "You think this guy will work with us if he finds out about Moses and Shed Harris?"

"I already told him we have community opposition. Today I'm going to lay it all out. He's accustomed to controversy. I think he thrives on being booed offstage at Columbia and Howard. That why he goes back. Drives the whi-whi's and gimme's crazy. But he gets respect from the black business community. He's got YouTube videos that get a lot of buzz. I see the links on a lot of corporate websites."

Brooks glanced at his Rolex and motioned to Winfield, "We should be there in ten minutes. Why don't you go back and tell the others to check their presentations one more time? And send Bijan up here. I need to go over some figures with him. As soon as we land, Tommy Steinman will take delivery of the plane. We sign a few forms, get our check, and grab a limo. We're supposed to meet Veraswami at the Trade Mart at five."

"Sure thing." Winfield unsnapped his seat belt and edged past Brooks to enter the passenger cabin. Whoever had defaulted on the IRS had megalomaniac tastes. The navy blue carpeting was bordered with gold stars and bore an eagle logo that gave the jet the look of a baby Air Force One. Bijan was checking stock tips in an investor newsletter. Winfield tapped him on the shoulder and motioned him forward. Hunched over laptops and calculators, Lionel, Keisha, Ted Kaleem, and Carlos muttered to themselves like law students cramming for the bar exam. From time to time they sipped Diet Coke or Perrier. The six pack of Horicon Springs Mineral Water, a gift from a bottler seeking venture capital, remained untouched. Winfield bravely took a bottle and strapped himself in to review his notes. The mineral water tasted faintly of Listerine. Chewing sticks of Carefree to kill the flavor, he gazed out the window. Through the clouds, he caught a glimpse of Lake Pontchartrain. Arriving in New Orleans in a Lear jet to take a limo to the International Trade Mart, Winfield felt a world away from car loan flyers and the basement Xerox machine.

The Top of the Mart dazzled with light. Seated at an immense table, Singh Veraswami, dressed in Saville Row pinstripes, waved to Brooks and Win as they got off the elevator.

Shielding his eyes from the sunbeams, Winfield watched Veraswami rise in greeting, his small, lean body silhouetted against the blazing gold afternoon sun. Walking across the red-carpeted bar, Brooks whispered to Winfield, "This is it. Let's hope we can swing it."

"I see you found me," Veraswami smiled broadly, his gold crowns gleaming. "I always choose this place for business meetings. The location is unmistakable, and the view of the city makes up for dull conversation. Please, please, sit down. The drinks are on me. When I come to Milwaukee, you can treat me at the Pfister. I love places with a view." Sweeping his hands like a symphony conductor, he gestured the group to circle round the table. A waitress in her forties, statuesque and blonde enough to have danced at the Sho-Bar in Win's youth, took their orders.

Clearing his throat, Brooks orchestrated the introductions. "Dr. Veraswami, I'm glad you have the opportunity to meet our whole team. I think you'll find Frederick Douglass shares a lot of the philosophies you outline in your book. First, there's my brother Lionel who is home taking care of business. He got his CPA two years ago and handles finance. This is Keisha Jackson. She's an attorney who specializes in real estate. Her father runs a civil law firm that's strong in class action and medical malpractice. Ted Kaleem has a BA from Cornell. He was a linebacker there, that's football. He has an MBA and was with the FBI for ten years. He's our expert in security and computer fraud. Bijan Naboti has a business degree from Teheran University and a Ph.D. from Wisconsin. He specializes in offshore investments, international law, and foreign trade. Carlos Sanchez has a doctorate in economics and does research on small business development."

As he listened, Veraswami's smile widened. Shaking hands, he held each person's gaze like a vaudeville mind reader as Brooks ran down their credentials. "This is Winfield Payton. He has a Ph.D. in English and has just agreed to be our Director of Communications."

Veraswami gently pumped Winfield's hand and winked. "Payton. Strange. When I saw your name, I assumed you would be black."

Brooks laughed, then leaned inward to speak more softly. "Winfield brings another asset to our team. He can be our chiclet."

"Chiclet?" Veraswami asked, cocking his head in curiosity.

"Our token white. He can go undercover for us, be our team's inconspicuous white face, our *Fortune* 500 front if you will."

"An important asset for a minority firm," Veraswami smiled. "Well, pleeze, let us all sit down."

Taking his chair, Winfield could not resist looking toward the French Quarter, mentally counting up half a dozen blocks to locate Bourbon Street. Under those shabby green roofs bosomy blondes were gyrating, spinning tassels with the fury of speedboat propellers. Sipping his drink, he recalled that long lost July. Perhaps he could return on spring break with enough money to take a suite at the Royal Orleans and treat a dancer or two to steaks at the Rib Room.

"Well, Dr. Veraswami," Brooks began, "we have all read your book about liberation capitalism and think a lot of your ideas match what we are attempting to do at FDI, the investment arm of Frederick Douglass Savings and Loan. We're small, but we have a strong team. We build on your concept of marshaling human resources. Everyone here, except me, of course, has a regular but flexible job. They have a base salary, benefits, a pension. That means we have a top team with little overhead. We can afford to compete with the big firms, undercut their prices, and deliver the same quality. Probably better. We're hungry, but not des-perate. The profits added to their existing salaries gives our team a Fortune 500 income without the risk. You see, it's right out your book. The chapter called 'False Dilemmas.'"

"That it is," Veraswami smiled. "The black man . . .," he paused, nodding to Keisha, ". . . and the black woman have long been presented with false dilemmas. Either you get a job and assimilate to vanish into the melting pot, or you maintain your authenticity through embracing ignor-ance, defiance, and poverty. Either you sell out to IBM and enrich yourself, or you forgo wealth and work in some community based non-profit, no-progress agency to help your people. As you suggest, there is no reason why we can't achieve both ends.

"You see, only capitalism can liberate us—but only if we free ourselves to embrace the opportunity. Islam teaches that it is the accumulation of wealth that separates man from the animal. True, Jesus likened the rich man's chances of getting into heaven to the camel's ability to pass through the eye of a needle. But Jesus spoke in the pre-capitalist era, at a time when rich men merely acquired and amassed wealth in the form of coin and treasure. But how Christian it is to invest! Think of the poverty, the disease, the distress one evaporates by achieving capital and investing it, allowing that wealth to create jobs, finance research in new technologies, and produce an income that is suitably taxed to support the poor. Only when Israel abandoned Zionist-socialism for techno-capitalism could it afford to absorb a million Russian immigrants. Promise them homes, jobs, a future. The Palestinians can throw stones in jealous anger or realize that cyberspace is more valuable than geography. It is duty of the liberal man and woman of conscience to become rich! In enriching ourselves, think of those we help!"

Veraswami spread his small smooth palms over the circle of whiskey glasses like a conjurer, "You see there are billions of dollars floating through the air. Billions. Money moves about us like hordes of migratory birds seeking a safe place to light. Billions every minute are transferred from one investor to another, moving from one nation to another," he continued, sounding like Carl Sagan counting stars. "Switzerland is a landlocked country with few natural resources. Yet it is prosperous by just banking other people's money. It is simply a trusted funnel. A safe storehouse. One needs only a small processing fee, a handling charge, to make millions from massive investments. But our young people walk about listening to rap music, the tribal grunts of the disaffected. They should be listening to the music of the spheres, the music of money. Instead of downloading tunes, they should be checking the markets. They are consumers only, embracing only one side of the equation. They see themselves as victims. They seek recognition through mere consumption. In New Orleans a minister organized protests outside a Nike store. 'Businessmen who sell shoes to our children for two hundred dollars a pair should put something back into the community,' he said to the media. He was serious, quite serious about that statement. I called him and told him, they already have put something back. Shoes! He was non-plussed. Unable to conceive! In his mind mere consuming must be rewarded. I asked him why he wasn't teaching these children to produce, to serve, to create, to sell. Design and sell their own shoes! Sell them online nationwide, worldwide. If he channeled the energy of his protesters into a platoon of salesmen or telemarketers, think of the money they could have generated!

"I encounter such limited imaginations every day! No concept of the army of opportunities available to us. In the past our leaders have seen progress in terms of factories, of material construction. But all we need is to become a funnel, a temporary parking spot offering security and a slightly higher return than the corner bank. We do that through diversification and profit sharing. Your firm is a perfect model. We eliminate the overhead of executive payrolls and benefits and work simply for profits. We share the wins and losses, investing time, insight, energy, as well as capital."

The waitress returned, and Winfield ordered a double. The table had rotated toward the Mississippi, which gleamed in the late afternoon sun. Blinking, Winfield reached for his drink, noting how the sunbeams transformed the ice cubes into gold nuggets.

"You see the problem with the black man is that he has always sought salvation from white men with beards. Think of it—Jesus, Mohammed, Marx, Freud, Lenin, your Lincoln, even more recently Castro and Che. Instead of seeking direction from within, he seeks approval from without."

Winfield sensed the lounge's rotation picking up speed. Hurricane-battered, the bar moved creakily. He sipped his whiskey as Veraswami spun on. "The problem with our leaders is they have no concept of what a job is. Al Sharpton argues for jobs as if they can be handed out like blocks of surplus cheese. They have no understanding that a job is not given, it is earned. One is not a recipient of a job—one must give, not take.

"Last year at one of my seminars I met a businessman from the Bronx. An admirable fellow. He hires as many young blacks as he can. But even the gifted students recommended to him by teachers and clergymen appall him by their ignorance of the market. For instance, at interviews he hands applicants a piece of paper and tells them to write down the salary they want. Whatever they want. Ten dollars an hour or a million a year. He then asks them to multiply that number by three. 'I can pay you the first number,' he says, 'provided you can produce the second. Go home and figure out how you can bring that much into our firm to earn your salary.' All he asks is that they generate more than they consume. You must create wealth before you can claim any right to it. But these gifted young people look back at him stumped, blank-faced, unable to conceive!

"They only know the right of consumption, the right of need. I need, therefore I deserve. It should be I produce, therefore I deserve. Teach our community that, and you can end poverty in a generation. We command the means. The reins are in our hands every day. African-Americans command the tenth largest economy in the world—yet how many buy from a black business or invest in a black bank? They decry the white man, yet as soon as they get a check, they rush off to white shopping malls to spend their money. If only it could be channeled!"

Veraswami leaned over the table, tapping its polished surface for emphasis, "We have abandoned our children to the secular left with its philosophy of zero-sum economics. We have reduced our children to aggrieved recipients who learn to justify themselves by their deficits, not their energy or imagination. Think of it, we tell them that to get a scholarship, to get benefits, to get a loan, they must demonstrate their poverty, not their talent, not their wealth. The harder off they are, the better. We tell society give us because we need, not because we can contribute."

Winfield sipped his drink. Having not eaten, it did not take much alcohol to make his head spin. The slight motion of the restaurant enhanced his disorientation. Veraswami's soft accent was seductive and addictive. No wonder his videos were popular.

"The color of liberation is green. The future challenges us to expand wealth while saving our environment. At present eight percent of the world's population owns cars. In America it is fifty-six percent. Where shall we be when the rest of the world catches up? A billion more cars! The need for environmental devices, for new fuels, for reprocessing junked vehicles will increase. Think of the need for parking in China and Russia! Think of India! In a few years its population will be greater than China's. Already its middle class is larger than the entire population of the United States. Consider their hunger for automobiles. One can become rich by simply building parking structures in Mumbai. But do we teach our children these opportunities, the opportunities in their own neighborhoods? Only recently in Harlem I talked with a young entrepreneur who was in the business of removing graffiti. At first, he and his friends went to shopkeepers and offered to clean and repaint their buildings for a fee. Then he got the idea of selling the space to local merchants, to ad agencies, city departments. Now he hires the youngsters who used to spray obscenities to paint murals for black merchants, for the NBA, for warnings about AIDS and drugs. This young man is remarkable, but he is eighteen and leaving for college. Think if we could motivate ten others who could motivate ten more!"

Brooks leaned forward. "Dr. Veraswami, we feel we have to be totally frank about one thing. We've sent you our mission statement, our financials, our personal and corporate profiles. But we do face opposition from some people in the community. Principally from two sources."

He swallowed hard, then continued. "Because Brewer's Court is considered part of the central city, it falls under the purview of the Inner City Redevelopment Commission. Now this is a purely non-governmental agency, a social organization only, but it does receive county and city funding and is politically influential. The director is a minister, but he is not the real problem. Shed Harris is. . ."

"Shed?" Veraswami asked, slightly amused by the name.

Ted Kaleem smiled grimly. "They say it stands for Shit Happens Every Day. He's a real Demi-More. You know, Democrats who only know word, 'More!'"

Veraswami shook his head, chuckling.

"Sadly, the name fits," Brooks continued. "He is a rabble-rouser. He is an old time liberal, a socialist. He is against this project because he's paranoid about gentrification. He condemns white flight, but when whites move back to the city, he calls them invaders. To be honest, we're personal enemies. He has a column in the community newspaper and denounces us every week for not being black enough, for selling out, for serving too many white interests."

Veraswami nodded. "I know the type."

"Well, he sits on the commission. You can count on him raising questions, organizing protests, and staging demonstrations. But he is almost benign next to Father Moses—he's our real worry. He's an inner-city alderman who sits on the commission and has the political clout to block everything from zoning to tax rebates."

"I've seen his website," Veraswami sighed. "Shameful."

Brooks twisted his glass on its gold coaster. "I tell you all this so you can be prepared. I think you should be aware of the downside, so that you're not taken unawares. In fact, I can understand why you might wish to decline our offer."

Veraswami waved his hand, rising in his chair. "These personalities are the blight of our times. Every city has its local crop of race tyrants. Ideological clowns! Race is the last refuge of the manic-depressive. These are people who cannot succeed in the mainstream, could never be elected to an office by promising to lower taxes or improve services. Instead, they shake their dreadlocks and flaunt tribal regalia and achieve status by defying the white man. Children."

"But they can sabotage our efforts," Brooks said. "They can scare off investors and political support. And we are going to have to ask the city for major tax breaks."

"Of course, that's just want Moses wants," Keisha argued. "If he can eliminate minority participation, then he can attack Brewer's Court for being lily white. Dr. Veraswami, you can't imagine how personal his attacks can be. He has been especially vicious toward Brook's brother Lionel."

Brooks lowered his head.

Veraswami nodded. "I was forced to leave Nigeria. My opponents accused me of everything from incest to infanticide. I was accused of sodomy and selling African children to the CIA for AIDS experiments. These people can only throw mud.

"You see progress is their enemy. They derive power from the impotent and the angry. They tell their followers they can achieve nothing without their leadership. Black men and women like yourselves threaten them; you present alternatives people like Moses fear. We must counter them at every point. But we must understand why people turn to them. They are afraid. They are ignorant. The race tyrant tells them that they can never make progress, and if they do, they are denounced as traitors.

"The argument of assimilation or separatism is specious. There will always be black neighborhoods in our cities, yet why must they be hostile camps? Think of Chinatown in San Francisco! We could walk down Grant Avenue—all of us strangers. All around us people would be speaking a language we could not understand. We would be surrounded by signs we could not read, strange sights, different smells! Yet, would we be afraid? Would we be shunned? Tourists flock by the thousands to walk that street every day. Think of the jobs that generates. Whole generations have lived there, separate but prosperous. Can we say the same of South Central or Harlem? And why not? Why can't our neighborhoods welcome tourists of all races! Think of the shops, the food, the fabrics, the music! Instead of seeing whites as enemies, we should see them as clients, customers, tourists.

"Capitalism is our salvation. Call it greed if you must, but at least greed makes you a creator, a builder, a seller. Need reduces you to begging. Our children are natural entrepreneurs. Hence the appeal of the gangs and dealers. We need only embrace them and light the path. So many others have faced what we face, the Italians, the Jews, the Irish," he said, glancing at Win.

Winfield took his cue. "When my great-grandfather came to this country, the only job he could get was sweeping the street. Back then the want ads, the sign-up sheets, the notices in the labor halls all said No Irish Need Apply. They often just abbreviated it to N. I. N. A. Those notices made him so mad he vowed that someday he would make a million dollars and name his daughter Nina. Well, he made three million and named his three daughters Nina—they had to go by their middle names. Nina Maureen Payton, Nina Bridget Payton, Nina Kathleen Payton."

Veraswami smiled warmly, leaning over to tap Win's shoulder. "You see," he said, turning to the others, "even our Irish chiclet has a lesson for us. Opportunities abound. We must only have the courage to embrace them. *Slainte!*"

Winfield sipped his Jameson. Embrace was an important verb in Veraswami's world. He had the table captivated. His gold cufflinks dazzling in the sunlight, Veraswami resembled a charming leprechaun, a guru banker encouraging everyone to have faith in the money wheel, the ebb and flow of capital. He spoke of stocks, bonds, and debentures the way a cardinal might invoke papal doctrines. In Winfield's mind the stock exchange began to assume the religious significance of the Vatican, a modern Mecca where all races were welcome to worship and prosper. His head spinning, he sipped more whiskey, the gold nuggets kissing his lips.

As promised, the flight back was not comfortable. The repoed DC-3 had all the amenities of a distressed school bus. There was a narrow steel bench with seatbelts. But after takeoff, everyone moved to the deck, bundling themselves in blankets and sleeping bags. The heat vents were no larger than those on a '68 Volkswagen. A string of glaring light bulbs swung back and forth, casting shadows. Rotating above New Orleans an hour before, the team from Frederick Douglass Investments looked like high flyers. Now, huddled in a rusting metal tube, shivering in surplus parkas, they resembled trapped coal miners awaiting rescue.

Winfield tried to sleep, but it was too chilly. He rummaged through his briefcase for something to read and encountered a folder of ungraded themes. Damn! He'd forgotten all about the thirty-odd papers he promised to evaluate for the Hillside Community Center. Brooks, eager to prove his staff's social commitment, asked everyone to volunteer. Win offered to tutor GED students.

The week before he had given the class a take-home assignment:

Today many people are concerned about their health. Write a paragraph describing what people can do to stay healthy.

Winfield took one of the essays at random and began to read, his fingers stiffening with cold:

> The best thing you can do to stay
> healthy is have no friends. Because
> fiends can get you killed. Like if you
> have a friend and he in a gang. You be
> walking down the street and someone see
> you and think you in the gang and shoot
> you. My brother went out to the store
> after school to get some stuff. My mother
> give him money to get some shredded wheet
> and milk. My brother he had a freind who
> brother in a gang. So they see him coming
> form the store and they shoot him in the
> head.
> My brother he was twelve years old.

GIMME SHELTER

"I've ordered two more cases of Asti," Lionel announced, consulting his leather-bound executive planner. "That should be enough. Twelve jugs of Chablis. Six Rhine. Ten rosé. Ten red. Miller's giving us five cases of Lite and three cases of Sharp's. Win, you ordered the water, right?"

"The distributor donated ten cases."

"Ten cases!" Lionel shook his head. "We don't want to drown anybody."

"Probably the only product they'll move in Milwaukee this year," Ted Kaleem muttered. "That was not the best venture capital scheme. Horicon Springs Mineral Water. Christ! Horicon Marsh is a waterfowl sanctuary. How can you call a mineral water Horicon? Makes everybody in Wisconsin think of swamp water and goose shit."

"It tastes as good as Perrier," Lionel insisted. "And they're coming up with a new label. One without a bird on it."

"It's selling in California," Keisha added hopefully.

"OK," Brooks said, "We've got the beverages lined up. Kresson is donating the buffet. He promised Leo will be doing the supervising. No more screw-ups like the Urban League dinner. I told him I gotta have some brothers doing more than slicing prime rib and stacking napkins. And we'll have a vegetarian line. Organic and gluten-free."

Ted flipped through his notepad. "Security is as tight as we can get it. I don't expect any problems. Parking lot surveillance is top priority. Can't afford to have any investors carjacked."

Brooks nodded. All the dot matrix boxes on his planning sheet were checked off three times—once in pencil and twice in ink, blue and red. Frederick Douglass Savings and Loan was set. In two weeks, the one-hundred-and-eighty-two-million-dollar Brewer's Court project would be announced to investors.

Bijan raised his hand. "I just wonder if we can expect any trouble from our good friends on the Inner City Redevelopment Commission. A demonstration? Picketing?"

Brooks pursed his lips, nodding, "Ted, any word on the street?"

"Right now those gimme's are too busy hustling the mayor for next year's budget. Word is they are late on their grant proposal. Hector Marquez is leaving to be treasurer of the Minority Chamber of Commerce. Cesar says most of the Hispanics are going to follow. That gives Shed some problems. He's gotta make more squeaks to get the grease. He might pull something just to get attention—to show folks he's still a player."

Brooks tapped his chin with the cap of his fountain pen. "OK, OK, it wouldn't hurt to create a low level diversion for the twenty-first. The school board meets that night. Maybe we can deflect some attention that way."

Ted smiled. "I'll sound out Leotha. She can put something on the minority teachers' website."

"Some parents are concerned about the university pulling out of the Bridge to Success program," Winfield added. "I read about that yesterday. Could be an issue."

"Right. Let me get Leotha on this. I don't think we should be involved. She can make a few calls. We don't want anything too big or too loud, just a few pickets to keep the gimme's and Demi-More's out of our hair. If we get them pumped to picket the school board meeting, they might just forget about us." Ted leaned back smiling, "You can't be in two places at once."

Lionel twisted his bow tie and leaned over the oak conference table, "What about Moses?"

"Oh, Christ," Ted moaned.

"Would he try anything?" Win asked softly. Moses was not a man to be trifled with. Eager for publicity, Alderman Moses recently took to brandishing a Zulu war shield at campaign rallies, giving press conferences in maladroit Swahili, and sponsoring a petition to have his district secede from the City of Milwaukee to become New Kemet, the first independent African nation in urban America. He claimed to have approached Ghana for diplomatic recognition. Whether clad in an assortment of tribal costumes no African had worn in a century or a forbidding Papa Doc black suit and Amish hat, bearded Moses was made for television. He had earned a national reputation, and the local media covered his every move, hoping their shots and sound bites might be picked up by FOX.

"God knows what he will come up this time," Ted sighed. "Maybe a mock lynching. Ever since he made *PrimeTime* by blowing whistles at Jimmy Carter rehabbing houses in the ghetto, he sees himself as a mover. Face it, Moses wants the gimme's to understand one thing—'yo down a hole, and I gots the only ladder in town.'"

"Let's not forget the Muslim angle," Winfield said. "I think Singh's presence may dampen some of the protest.

After all, he's no Donald Trump. How can anyone object to having African investors?"

"That's true," Ted said, his brow furrowing with displeasure. "But we're going for maximum press coverage. We've got national black press coming. That's enough to make Moses rut."

"Win, what about local TV?" Brooks asked.

"Channels Twelve and Six are on board for sure," Winfield said. "Let's just hope a Russian coup or a plane crash doesn't bump us off the air. Sedlov has promised a big spread in the Sunday business section with pictures. BET may send a crew; they're taping in Chicago the day before and promised to come if they can. I offered to send a limo to pick them up and have them stay at County Galway. The hotel rooms are on me. O'Brien owes me a favor. He's got two rooms for the twenty-first. And I have a film student shooting video we can package for cable distribution or cut up for podcasts."

Brooks' Mount Blanc scratched off the last dot matrix box a fourth time for emphasis.

"Well, guys, I don't think we can do anymore until Wednesday night. We pull this off, and we're on our way. National players. No more tavern loans and duplex mortgages. We'll have a base of investors to leverage." He raised both hands and crossed his fingers. "It's after six, let's break for dinner. We all have a long day tomorrow. Win, how about joining Lionel and me? We're heading to the Casbah."

Winfield nodded, his stomach clenching at the thought. Another meal at a client's. He wondered why so many pseudo-North African restaurants had opened in Milwaukee. Operated by the Diaspora of Palestine and the South Bronx, these converted discos and renovated daycare centers featured Moorish arches, ceiling fans, blazing New Wave neon, and sickly palm trees in brass pots. And all the food was black—black bean soup, blackened salmon, blackened steak, pepper-encrusted lamb, and black rice drenched in charcoal-flavored teriyaki sauce.

"The Casbah has a salad bar, doesn't it?" Win asked.

"Sure thing," Lionel said, "but the blackened chicken is the best. Get the special with bitter-chocolate and almond sauce and the caramelized yams."

Caramelized yams! Winfield thought of Dr. Tanner, the Victorian lecturer who espoused total fasting. He claimed to have a patient who had not touched food in fourteen years. He must have seen a Casbah menu.

Balancing desire with discretion, Winfield judiciously plucked a few corrugated carrot sticks from the salad bar and added them to his plate of limp lettuce strewn with slices of petrified turkey and strips of shiny ham. He found a few semi-crisp celery spears and a lone edible radish. Ignoring the ceramic bowls of clotted dressing and rancid bacon bits, Winfield returned to the table and ordered a double Jameson. Whisky and salad always go well together. The booze gave the cold vegetables a smoky warmth. Far different from the fresh garden salads he ordered at Twin Oaks to accompany an after-school martini. Tanqueray gave everything a delicate pine-flavor.

Brooks carefully dissected his blackened herbal chicken, carving through the seared crust to reveal strips of darkened but still unburnt flesh. Chewing energetically, he started to speak, then raised his palm for a pause as he swallowed and winced. "Win, do you think we can pull it off?"

"If Singh can get us ten to twenty million from new investors, why not?"

"I can't wait for this to be over. We should know by Friday. I figure if we don't hear any opposition by the end of the week, we should be home free."

Brewer's Court. Winfield smiled. Having slaved for weeks over the text accompanying the glossy pictures for a battery of promotional booklets and blogs, Winfield had memorized all the details. Given enough investor capital and public support needed for zoning changes, the old abandoned brewery on the banks of the Milwaukee River would be transformed into a European hamlet within walking distance of the central business district. Yuppies, Buppies, and Wanna-be's with credit could live in energy-efficient, high-tech condos featuring saunas and secure parking, sip espresso in a bay-windowed Starbucks, stroll cobbled streets, or open offices on the upper floors of the remodeled malt house. The ornate warehouse would camouflage a 300 car garage offering plenty of free parking for retail customers.

"It's a big step for us," Winfield said.

"Especially for you, pal. We pull this off and you can think about setting up your own consulting firm. All the retailers will need promo work. We'll need brochures to sell the condos. We can even open an S&L branch. Think of the built-in clientele."

Win chewed his carrots carefully. Tension was mounting, welling inside him. He would have a sleepless night, even though his work was over. It was too late to make any changes or additions. The slick press kits, the impressive investor pamphlets were already packed for delivery. The website, with its virtual walking tour and 3-D architectural model, was registering six hundred hits a day.

There was nothing to do but wait. In the meantime, he needed to unwind. Crunching the last of his carrots, he excused himself and walked through the Moorish arches to the men's room to use his smart phone.

Two hours later, eyes closed, he felt soft cool fingertips brush his temples and run down the sides of his neck. Barbie tentatively massaged his shoulder. Winfield winced.

"I hope you didn't pull a muscle."

"I'm OK," Winfield muttered, clenching his teeth. It had taken a hundred swats with a studded leather paddle to coax Barbie into a ball-gag muted orgasm.

"I wanted to go for two," she said, "but I know topping takes a lot of energy. Being a bottom, I just have to get on my knees and feel. But tonight, I dunno, my focus just wasn't there. But I owe you one. Care for some oral?" she asked, like an Appleby's server told to push the desserts.

The lobby of the Alhambra Hotel, its canopy of gold-leafed moldings, recently patched and painted, slowly began to fill. Tugging at his bowtie, Lionel surveyed the main bar where red-jacketed black men swiftly and silently produced drinks with robotic precision. Waiters moved gracefully through the crowd, carrying napkin-covered bottles of Horicon Springs to reticent Baptists.

Winfield mingled, shaking hands, greeting acquaintances, and counting faces. Clicking his teeth to keep a mental score, he noted two aldermen, a state senator, two former Congressmen, a covey of contractors, and a knot of cautious bankers. As instructed, he made his presence known to the restless group of white prospects. He shook hands, mentioned his father, and did all he could to lend a Caucasian tinge to Frederick Douglass Investments.

His role over, Winfield slipped into the ballroom and ascended the stage where a long row of tables had been erected. Brooks was moving about briskly, checking charts, and testing the video monitors. He glanced at Winfield, "Ready to go?"

"As ready as I'll ever be."

Winfield took his place and studied his notes. No college lecture, not even his dissertation defense, had made him this nervous.

Impressed by the red-carpeted glitz and video cameras, the guests, fueled by patriotically domestic champagne, began to assemble in the ballroom. Dressed in a flowing white robe fringed in gold, Dr. Veraswami walked across the stage to greet Winfield and Brooks with pressed palms and bowed head.

Brooks stood, adjusted his red power tie dotted with GOP elephants and addressed the room.

"Ladies and gentlemen, we are here tonight to unveil a piece of the future. This community, this country is facing a crisis. We must learn to create jobs and expand our economy without destroying our environment and worsening the deficit. We have to raise revenues to combat drugs, rebuild our cities, and care for our elderly without curbing free enterprise. Too often these issues are viewed in opposition. But if we are to prosper, we must achieve a balance and work together.

"Brewer's Court will increase the city's tax base by eighty million dollars, create 200 housing units within minutes of the central city, provide unique office and retail space, and create scores of new jobs. There are larger developments in this town, and there are grander rehab projects. But this marks a unique minority enterprise uniting African and African-American investors and entrepreneurs. This partnership has attracted interest on two continents and promises to be a catalyst for the twenty-first century."

Winfield glanced at his notes, calculating what tone to adopt. He was so absorbed that Lionel had to tap his knee twice to get his attention.

"Check out who just came in," he whispered.

Looking up, Winfield saw a bearded black man in a black rabbinical hat and belted jumpsuit lead half a dozen uniformed men to vacant seats in the back row. They wore dark glasses beneath black-visored Pullman caps and sat with arms crossed like Egyptian mummies.

Father Moses! The school board meeting ploy hadn't worked. Perhaps this was to be another silent protest. None of the men appeared armed with whoopee cushions—their customary weapons of choice used to disrupt the mayor's press conferences. The audience was still focused on Brooks. The elbowing and head-turning hadn't started. If I can only get through my presentation, Winfield prayed.

Brooks wound up to a finish and introduced Win, "Perhaps one of the most unique aspects of this redevelopment project is its commitment to community education and training. Dr. Winfield Payton, our Communications Director, will explain how Brewer's Court will create educational opportunities for minority youth."

The applause was more than polite. It lasted long enough for Win to shuffle through his notes and situate himself behind the podium.

"For the past twenty years," he began, "both the university and MITI have promised to make a meaningful contribution to inner city job development. A dozen plans have come and gone, but Brewer's Court provides the first real opportunity for these two institutions to help the community. The university has committed half a million dollars to create an educational partnership with MITI. Together, they will train minority job seekers and work directly with local employers. The construction and rehab will provide on-the-job training for twenty students in MITI's carpentry and plumbing program. Six minority architecture students will have a chance to learn the entire building process from design to construction. They will master...."

Winfield droned on, punctuating his remarks with words like "community," "investment," "hope," "progress," and "jobs" that scored high with the focus groups. Win had also tested them with his black students, weaving them into innumerable subject-verb agreement exercises and comma drills.

He talked on and on, gathering inspiration from the sea of upturned faces. Every time he said "jobs," he noticed the smiles widen, the eyes brighten. The audience was in the palm of his hand. He ran on auto pilot, his eyes sweeping over the intent, supportive faces in the front row. On the horizon of his vision the half-dozen black clad figures sat unmoving, stoic, lifeless.

Time was flying. He cut some details and went for the kill. "When completed, Brewer's Court will endure as a living monument of what we can do. It will preserve our heritage while pointing to our future. Brewer's Court will remind us that in the future when we work together almost anything we can imagine we can create..."

"Yo!"

He was being addressed. Winfield turned, at first detecting nothing but a moving blur in the back of the hall. Father Moses was standing. Tall. Massive. Bearded. In his black Amish coat and black rabbinical hat, he loomed over the audience like a demented John Brown. His voice boomed.

"Yo, people! Yo, people! Bruthers 'n Sistuhs! This was 'posed to be a Black Thang! A Black Thang! Building homes for the 'hood! Not some Yuppie palace for a bunch of crackers and Oreos, man! Read yo history, people, read yo history!

"That land was set aside when them German beer people who got tired of selling us malt liquor to kill our brains skipped town owing ten million in back taxes. The city set this land aside for low-income housing. Low-income! Not six-hundred-an'-fifty-thousand-dollar condos! Not three-thousand-dollar-a-month apartments! And not for no goddam Starbucks! Homes for the 'hood, not a bunch of wanna-be-whites and their bleach blonde 'hos.

"You know the type," he cried, fanning his hands over the crowd. "The type of black folk who look white, talk white, dress white, dream white. The type of black people who every time they vote Republican run to the baffroom 'n look in the mirror to see if they lightened up any. The type of black folk who wouldn't be caught dead eatin' fried chicken or catfish, no suh!"

"Sit down!" A voice shouted from the front row.

Winfield, his knuckles gone white on the podium, swallowed hard and felt his knees quiver. He glanced sideways. Ted Kaleem had left the wings. The off-duty cops he hired were slowly moving up the aisles.

"Sit down!" The speaker was a middle-aged black man in a double-breasted jacket. "I came here . . . I paid to come here to listen to a presentation, not attend a demonstration."

Moses drew himself to his full height and bellowed, "Don't none of you sheep see what's going on? Don't none of you niggers see at all? Check out them wanna-be's up there. Crook Adams and his faggit bruther Lyin' Nell. Check out their so-called dream team. You got that Desi Arnez Cuban dope dealer Carlos up there. That towel-head rug merchant Bijan somethin' or other. That New York Jew Waldheimerstein or whatever. Keisha Washington! That 'ho help raise fifty grand for Romney but not one dime for the community. And *Pay-ton*!"

Winfield's knees buckled like the Scarecrow's before the Wizard of Oz.

"*Pay-ton*! That muthah-fucker flunked my son in English! And that Very-Slimy Afican. He ain't nuthin' but a shoe-polished Englishman. He is from India. He ain't no real Affican! Hell, he whiter than Prince Charles. And you people lissen to his ass? Don't you know that when they was putting yo gran-daddy in the slave ship, his gran-daddy was standing on the dock counting his money? Who you think sold us? You think white men could go into the jungle and catch us? Hell, they played on the beach and chased pussy while them African high hats did all the dirty work"

"Shame! Shame!" An enormous woman was standing, waving a white handkerchief as if to dismiss an evil presence with an incantation. "Shame on you for your language! There are church people here."

"That may be, people. I offer you a vision, and it ain't got nothing to do with the horseshit being sold heah. Keep it real, people. Keep it real!"

Winfield found himself talking with the calm, assuring voice of an airline pilot announcing an unintended water landing. "There is no need for alarm. This presentation offers one vision of the future. One plan to repair one part of a single neighborhood. It doesn't cancel anyone else's plan. It does not prevent anyone else from making progress. We are simply trying—the best way we know how—to help make something positive happen. We may not succeed. There is a lot against us. But we're lighting a candle. You can snuff it out, or light your own."

The ministers in the front row were nodding, and for a moment Winfield wondered if he had missed his calling as a televangelist.

"That may be *Pay-ton*! Light yo' candle. Leastways you ain't hidin' yo honky hide behind some black mask. Hell, all you folks up there is white. White as Klan sheets. The only thang black you got is black hearts. Look at them people up there. That rainbow coalition of crooks. I know you all thinking how precious it is to see whites 'n blacks, Jews 'n Muslims, boys 'n girls all workin' and smilin' together," he continued in a sing-song voice. "Well, so what? They're too busy filling their pockets with the people's money to hate. Don't let a little color blind yo! The color of the people oppressing and rapin' yo don't matter! Don't let these house niggahs sell you out to their white massahs!" Moses stretched out his arms to the audience. "Lissen, people. You can all sit here and lissen to this shit and drink yo French champagne and write out yo checks and think yo doing something—or—you can come across the street and be down with the brothers. The Bruthers of Struggle who is locked up for nuthin. The sistuhs selling themselfs to white men to feed their kids. You can stay here or meet with us 'cross the street. We be real. Real food. Real music. Rap soul, people, not some faggity Bobby Short Wanna-be playing Cold Porter. But something with guts. Yo choice, people! Yo choice!" He raised his fist, "Keep it real, nigguhs! Keep it real!"

He turned and marched out, his followers filing quietly behind him. Brooks picked up a microphone and marched to the podium. "I think tonight we have seen why Brewer's Court is so important to our community. There seem to be two kinds of folks in this town. Those who wish to challenge the poor with opportunity and those who use them as a powerbase. We have to ask ourselves if we want to take pride in black accomplishments and be a vital force in our country or become nothing more than a sideshow of whining clowns as other people of color take our places at the table."

Confused applause spattered across the room, giving Winfield just enough cover to scurry to his seat. The media people were in a frenzy. They had just enough time to make the ten o'clock news.

After the audience settled down, Dr. Veraswami took the podium.

"My friends, oddly enough, this makes me feel very much at home. Nothing of consequence is accepted easily. Remember your own Civil Rights movement. The demand to simply sit at a lunch counter sparked riots. And yet, even in this country, where we are only a minority, black people have achieved so much more than in Africa. Yes, you honor Africa, you recall her past glory, but I know her sad present." His soft, British accent soothed the crowd. He smiled, spreading his palms in an all embracing gesture. "Recall the heartache of Biafra, the genocide in Rwanda. The conflict of our race is not eliminated by the absence of white people. We can either join together to build temples or squabble over spare change in the marketplace. The vision challenges us, frightens us. We must embrace the future if it to be ours. We are a great people. To proclaim this fact one need not denigrate any others. To claim that your wife is beautiful is no insult to other women. To say that we have the ability to achieve does not mean we must ostracize those of other races who share our vision. To protest against progress, to blindly adhere to tribal ways is like the child who wants the benefits of adulthood without the responsibilities. These antics of protesters are only a sad commentary on the immaturity of their vision. Like impatient children they stamp their feet, they bully, they huff, they puff. But, my people, we know better. The Jewish gangsters and Irish thugs who terrorized New York a century ago have evaporated into history. Dismissed and forgotten by their great-grandchildren—doctors, lawyers, bankers. Mr. Moses decries us as the enemy. One should hope that we, too, shall make progress, and these childish mobs will be forgotten. In the future I hope black school children will see his type only in a history book. They shall be the stuff of legend, but bearing no more influence on the young than Billy the Kid and Jesse James have on white freshmen at Yale or Harvard. The choice is ours."

The audience appeared soothed. Winfield, no longer feeling on the verge of collapse, sighed with the relief of the acquitted. When the presentation ended, he strolled easily to the lobby where knots of interested parties lingered around drinks and hors d'oeuvre. Waiters served coffee and amaretto. The pianist, evidently flattered by his comparison to Bobby Short, played a flamboyant version of "Night and Day." Winfield walked over to Brooks, and together they moved from group to group, shaking hands and sharing Moses stories. No one seem offended or intimidated. But the laughter was forced and nervous. For Win's benefit, the blacks told gross jokes about Moses' horde of illegitimate children, while the whites punctuated their comments with politically correct, obligatory "but-Moses-does-have-a-point" concessions.

Win and Brooks made the rounds and moved to the bar, deciding not to be too intrusive. Potential investors were pocketing flyers and watching videos. A crowd of drinkers stood around a poster-sized display of Brewer's Court. They elbowed each other, pointing out features of the architect's models.

"It's selling itself," Brooks smiled. "You did a good job on those promo packets. Look over there," Brooks pointed to a pair of Chicago bankers. "When people pull out their calculators, you know they're serious."

They were sipping Crown Royal and basking in the afterglow when the searchlights hit them. Shielding their eyes from the stabbing light, they moved to the windows, blinking in pain. Winfield donned sunglasses.

"What the hell is it?" Brooks asked, trying to peer through the window.

Ted Kaleem ran up to them, puffing, "It's Moses. I just came in from outside. He's across the street, holding a rally. Those lights are his."

"Did you call the police?" Brooks asked, wincing as he tried to get a better look.

"Already here, but there is nothing they can do. He's got a permit."

"Who issued him a permit?"

"He did. Signed it himself. He's still an alderman. Unless it starts to get ugly or someone waves a gun, the cops won't do a thing."

Brooks glanced around the lobby. "OK, OK, show everyone out the side doors—they're closer to the parking lot anyway."

Fleeing the light, potential investors headed for the exits, spilling drinks and littering the floor with discarded brochures. Winfield felt deflated. All his colorful flyers lay like fallen leaves on an October sidewalk.

"Oh, Christ, Win, listen," Brooks moaned.

Amplified by speakers, the voice of Moses rolled like thunder from across the street.

"People! Look at them fools over there. All them Oreos and crackers! We oughta take cookie cutters and do a Dahmer on 'em. Cut 'em up! Don't let them fools use your poverty to line their pockets. They take money for the poor to build houses for the rich. Trickle down they calls it! Trickle down! Well, I say, you don't piss on *my* people and call it rain!"

A crowd was gathering, hooting with delight. Black uniformed Moses supporters passed out fried chicken.

"Oh God, Win, let's get out of here fast," Brooks urged. "I wanted to celebrate tonight. Now all I want to do is run home and hide under the covers. Can you imagine what the media will say about this?"

They grabbed their coats, ducked down the stairs, and slipped out a side door to the alley. Moses had turned the platform over to a rap group chanting "Uzi! Uzi! Uzi!"

"God no, it's the Uzi's! I thought those guys were on the road," Brooks hissed. Winfield caught a glimpse of the leather-clad rappers in visored caps dancing atop a flatbed truck. The lead singer, microphone cupped to his mouth like a harmonica, paced back and forth, the backup singers joining him in chanting refrains:

> I rob me a house every day,
> I fuck white bitches, what kin I say?
>
> *Uzi! Uzi! Uzi!*
>
> You take ma cash, mess with ma stash,
> I gonna kick yo funky black ass.
>
> *Uzi! Uzi! Uzi!*
>
> Ya steal my crack, snatch my wife,
> Get me a rope, gimme a knife!
>
> *Uzi! Uzi! Uzi!*
>
> Cut you up just for fun,
> finish you off with my little Jew gun!
>
> *Uzi! Uzi! Uzi!*

Ted glanced up and down the alley. "OK, let's break for the parking lot. We gotta make sure we can get out of here. Keep your lights off and back up slowly, then peel out onto Third Street. Let's rendezvous at County Galway. If you run into trouble, call me. If it's really rough, hit 911."

They were moving among parked cars, when a searchlight found them.

Moses, flanked by bodyguards blocked the alley. "Let them have it! Stone them for their sins! Give them a sign! Give them a sign!" he beckoned.

Fists raised against the light. Objects hurled toward them. *Intifada!*

Win crouched beside his car, expecting to hear his windows shatter. Something exploded against the hood. Objects pelted his windshield. A black disc whizzed past his wrist. Another grazed the nape of his neck. Yanking open the door, he felt something sting his calf. Starting the engine, he hunched behind the steering wheel for protection as the fusillade intensified. Peering over the dashboard, he saw a line of dark figures racing forward, their windmilling arms firing objects as fast as machine guns. Ninja stars? The small black objects hit his car and exploded, breaking off into twin discs.

Oreo cookies!

Fifteen minutes later Winfield was downing his second shot of Jameson 1780. Surrounded by symphony-goers leisurely sipping Irish coffee, he felt flushed and out of place. Lionel shook his head, too shaken to notice the slim-hipped waiter who tossed his hair invitingly at any male who looked his way. Ted sighed. Bijan dejectedly swirled his Diet Coke. Raising his hand to order another round, Win felt something slip from his collar and land on the bar.

They all looked down.

Lionel picked up the sandwich cookie. "Look," he said, rubbing his thumb over the smooth surface, "they're not even real Oreos."

"CAN WE TALK?"

"Win, it's Lori. Can we talk?"

Turning from his computer, Winfield rubbed his eyes as he juggled the telephone.

"Win, you're the only person I can talk to. I've been going through a lot this week. Brit's in Atlanta, and I'm all alone. I don't feel comfortable in this house by myself. Can I come over? Just to talk. I know you're busy, so I won't stay long. I promise. Please?"

He agreed. Winfield had been thinking of taking a break and heading to The Black Shamrock for a soul-restoring Guinness. But it had been over two years since he had heard from Lori, and her pleading sounded particularly inviting and full of promise.

Hanging up the phone, Winfield settled back, loosened his tie, and glanced at the computer screen. The lettering seemed a blur. He had spent the entire day editing the third draft of a documentary screenplay. A wealthy UW alumna, impressed by *The Roosevelts*, had endowed the Wisconsin Presidential Project. But since Wisconsin had never produced a president, the best alternative her overpaid board of directors could suggest was to fund the state's leading presidential historian, UW's own Siobhan Sapperstein, who immediately called Win. Over shots of Jameson at an Irish Seder the year before, he had claimed he had a screenplay "being considered" by Time Warner. Politely impressed, she asked him for help to bring her four-volume 2400-page masterpiece *Warren G. Harding: Man of Destiny* to the small screen. Siobhan's enthusiasm for the 29th President was infectious, and Winfield spent weekends in her study poring over the collected papers—all sixteen volumes—of the Harding Administration, searching for memorable quotes. Late into the night they ate pizza and watched YouTube clips of silent black and white newsreels, selecting scenes to match their narration. Admittedly, Warren G. Harding was not JFK, and Siobhan Sapperstein was no Doris Kearns Goodwin, but with enough work and hype, their efforts to revive public interest in Teapot Dome and the President's mysterious death (they planned to darkly suggest an international conspiracy) would be seen on a smattering of PBS affiliates, maybe even the History Channel.

Deciding to switch from Diet Coke to whiskey, Win went to the living room and checked the bar. He hoped Lori still drank Scotch. There was a full Cutty and half-liter of JB left over from his birthday party.

Lori. He first met her in college. Busty, blonde, and playful, she was every freshman's dream. Lori. But she belonged solely to Frank. Football Frank. Fraternity Frank. Fidelity-demanding Frank. He glommed onto Lori during Rush Week, eclipsing Win's chances forever. Throughout college, Lori remained on Win's horizon, gliding past him in hallways, brushing up next to him at beer bashes, asking him for advice on term papers, and sitting next to him at graduation. Always busty, always smiling, always blonde, and always unobtainable.

Win ran into her in grad school, and they became fast, if distant, friends. Frank became a pal as well, asking Win for help writing a resume. Lori even asked Win to plan their European honeymoon.

Lori always remained out of his grasp. When she broke up with Frank, she moved in with two girls. Wherever she went, her friends followed. From time to time Lori invited herself to Win's apartment, her dreary, druggy divorcee roommates trooping behind her with six packs and Valium. As Lori and Win talked about the old days, her roomies shot sullen hate-men looks at Win, dropped Virginia Slims ashes on his Persian rugs, used his phone, soiled his guest towels, and effectively blockaded any romantic overtures. Lori loved to talk, and her roomies loved to nod in mutual understanding. When Lori left the room, there was deadly silence. The roomies talked to each other as if Win were nothing more than an abandoned houseplant.

Briefly Lori lived by herself in Downer Estates, often calling on Winfield for small favors. But as always she maintained a platonic distance. He felt his lust gradually cool to compassion. His own relationship with an airline pilot was rocky, and he called on Lori for insight into the female psyche. Bonded by confusion and frustration, they went to erotic films together, listened to Dr. Ruth, and came to discuss sex with such openness and intensity so that anything physical between them would be doomed to self-conscious failure. Yet, he still pined for her.

Pined for her even now. Even after she came out of the closet and began living with a woman. Twenty years removed from that freshman September, he still ached for her, despite her chain smoking, her whiny monologues, her lesbian crushes.

Lori arrived at ten-thirty, sweeping into his living room and immediately heading to the bar. She wore white. White thin-ribbed turtleneck sweater. White stirrup pants. White heels. Barbie had not dropped by for over a week, and Win's neglected manhood immediately throbbed with anticipation.

"Oh, Win," she sighed, making a Scotch and water, "I'm really going through a lot. Everything's just getting worse and worse!" Moving to the sofa, she leaned over and gave Winfield a gooey kiss on the cheek. "I really appreciate this. I need to talk. I've been going crazy all day sitting around the house. I just feel so confused when Brit is away. I get so lonely and worried about everything. And I was looking forward to this week because I wanted to grub around with no makeup, paint the kitchen, and do some gardening. But I can't relax. I just feel lonely and horny and scared. It's like I'm sixteen again."

Slipping off her heels, she moved to the sofa, folded her legs in a lotus position and gulped Scotch. "Oh, Win. I don't know where to begin. I'm going through so many changes. I'm seeing a therapist. The woman hates me. I pay hundred-ninety-five dollars an hour because she's not in my HMO, and she despises me. The woman is a bitch. She just sits there and says "mmm" and looks down her nose at me. I see her twice a week. I mean women are so judgmental. And men, forget it. Whenever I tried to talk to Frank he only listened long enough to unzip his pants. Win, you are the only one I feel comfortable with."

Win nodded, sadly accepting his status as eunuch mentor.

"When I was with Frank, I wasn't happy. The sex always bothered me. From a physical point of view, he was equipped. Well-equipped. But it never worked for me. I tried, but I usually faked it. He was working so hard at it, I felt obligated to do it for him. I didn't know what was wrong. I just couldn't get into it. I always thought about women, but when I went to the bars—eee—they were all so dikey."

She held her empty glass aloft. "I shouldn't drink. It's bad for your face. Makes you puffy. But I need it." She rattled her ice cubes for attention.

Win made her a stiff drink, pouring a stiffer one for himself.

"OK," she continued, "then I met Brit. Oh, Brit. I never thought I would meet anyone like her. What an angel. And she's so smart. She has that web design business and all those rental properties. Now she owns shares in a Florida hotel. And being with her was so different than being with Frank. For the first time I really felt free. I could share everything with her. I mean we both went through divorces. We both wanted to be models. We both love to travel. But it's not working lately. I've sensed her pulling back. And I started faking it with her. I know she is faking it with me."

She took a hard pull at her drink. "Lately, I have been dreaming about being with a man again. Not Frank. No, not Frank." She glanced at Winfield for a moment. "And it's not you. It's this guy I ran into at Kinko's. He's so muscular. What a hard body! I've been thinking about what it would be like to be him. I guess I miss that."

Despite her Kinko's infatuation, Lori's admission of phallic deprivation restored Win's masculine ego a bit, and he put his drink down.

"And there is something else bothering me more and more. I'm thirty-seven. I'm thinking about kids, and my time is running out. I was never into the baby thing, but I always could do it if I wanted to. It was always an option. Now I'm scared of losing something."

She downed the last ounce of Scotch and held her glass up to Winfield. "I shouldn't drink on top of pills, but I can't relax." She stood, stretched, and followed Win to the bar. He was getting boozy. Fatigue pulled at his eyelids. It was going to be a long night.

"The thing is, Win, I'm still a housewife. OK, I work. I make good money in sales. But Frank had his own software company. And Brit, my God. Today I got ten calls for her from Dallas, LA, New York, Tampa. It's like being with

Frank. I play secretary. I take her messages. I check her email. I go to her conventions, just like with Frank, but she won't go to mine, just like with Frank. I was always intimidated by Frank. Now it's the same with Brit. I'm afraid she'll meet some twenty-year-old mall kitten and dump me. Oh, Win, it's always something."

Coffee. Win sipped and listened, his mind overloaded. It was nearly two am. He was exhausted and Lori—thankfully, thankfully—was finally winding down. Dozing, his head bobbed like Reagan's during a cabinet meeting. When Lori excused herself to use the bathroom, his eyes closed and he rocked forward, almost pitching into the glass coffee table. He woke with a start, catching his balance just in time.

Lori returned, yawning.

Time for bed. Winfield crossed the room, took Lori's arm and guided her into the bedroom. He pulled back the comforter, then began to undress. Lori slipped off her pants, leaving on her sweater and pantyhose. She climbed into bed. Win snapped out the light, sleep having overcome any erotic urges. Lori wrapped a smooth thigh over his and nuzzled close to him, her breasts jutting under Winfield's chin. Lori's small palm stroked the bulge in his briefs. Winfield sighed, gave her a brotherly hug and settled into his pillow to dream.

Lori sat up, knocking Winfield against the headboard. "Win, this just won't work. I can't sleep. I have to talk."

He rose, snapping on the light.

"No, Win. I feel so embarrassed unloading all of this on you. But I have to talk to somebody. Look, you're tired. Can I use your phone? I need to talk."

Win pointed to his study.

"Sleep, darling, I won't bother you." Planting a soft kiss on his cheek, she switched off the light and walked through the bathroom, closing both doors behind her. Alone in the darkness, Win drifted. He dreamed. His consciousness rose and fell on ocean waves, moving from coma-like stupor to light awareness of Lori's voice. Her whispers, stifled giggles, tearful sobs penetrated his dreams. Toward dawn, Winfield awoke. His normal morning state of arousal was particularly intense, stimulated no doubt by the choked orgasmic moans coming from his study.

A few minutes later Lori crawled into bed with him. Gazing at him with a blissful smile, she sighed and closed her eyes. She pulled closer, nuzzling her breasts under his chin. When her exploring hand encountered him, she offered a whispered rebuke and a sleepy, patronizing frown, "Oh, Win."

They slept until ten. After a cold shower, Winfield made coffee and toast. Lori was all apologies.

"Win, I want to make this up to you. Come over for dinner. Brit will be home in two days. She likes you. Maybe Saturday? We're going to have friends over. And I want you to feel welcome. I appreciate the fact you didn't try anything last night, not even hint at it. I mean that's class. Most men just aren't that understanding. My sister went to a therapist for marital problems, and the guy exposed himself. Right in his office on Park Avenue. In front of his bust of Freud and his aspidistras and everything. I mean this guy was on *The Doctors* talking about trust and commitment, and the first time my sister sees him, he pulls it out. And he wasn't even hung. I mean if you're going unreel your hose in public have at least eight inches. Otherwise, it's just pathetic."

That weekend Winfield joined Lori and Brit for a pool party. No fewer than four very straight-but-tired-of-being-hit-on-by-jerks females were in attendance wearing only thongs. Lori introduced Win, profusely praising him, and by the third round of low-cal wine coolers, he had collected two promising Skypes.

Three weeks later when he opened his phone bill, Winfield assumed there had been a computer error, a misplaced decimal. It was impossible, despite his calls to Wall Street for Frederick Douglass Savings and Loan, his weekly call to his parents, and the FAX's he sent to the Wisconsin Presidential Project, to have run up a $612.97 bill in a single month. He was about to call customer service for an explanation when his eye caught the dot matrix lines under ADDITIONAL CHARGES:

    10/12   2:21 am   1-900-555-8989
CHATLINE
        WOMYN TO WOMYN LINE
     138 min $3.99 $550.62
      4:40 am   1-900-555-9595
CHATLINE
        STUD LINE 900
      3 min $1.99 $5.97

THE PRIZE

Nothing is sadder than October snow. Winfield stood at his office window, watching the flakes sweep past C262, each one an omen of a long and bitter winter. It would take another two decades for global warming to tame the subzero winds that would soon whip off Lake Michigan. Win glanced across the snow-swept street at the college's main building. Unlike the palatial "Old Main's" that grace liberal arts colleges from Vermont to California, MITI's main building was a monument to WPA practicality. Filling an entire city block, the six-story bulwark was grimmer than KGB headquarters. Dark, soot-grimed, sullen, depressing, it dominated State Street like a fortress.

Yet this besmudged Bastille housed the board room, the president's suite, and the deans' offices—those soft-lit, plush carpeted, wood-paneled rooms decorated with flags, dried flowers, Erte prints, and gold-framed portraits of long-dead Germanic mayors. From these offices flowed jobs, consulting contracts, per diem research assignments, paychecks, benefits, and pensions. As an instructor, Winfield regarded this dark structure with favor, gazing on its dirty bricks like a nineteenth-century mogul contemplating a steel mill.

And today was pay day.

His check would include 27.5 hours of professional assignment pay for writing a grant proposal. An extra seventeen hundred dollars. Even after deductions, there would be almost another thousand in the net pay box. An extra thousand. Money for another block of stock or a nice addition to his down payment fund. After five years in Downer Estates, Winfield was ready to leave a singles' complex for a real home, a condo in Brewer's Court.

The snow had stopped when Win left his last class, his briefcase stuffed with creative writing exercises. Laboring under the influence of alcohol, methadone, Valium, and Prozac, his students produced aphasic paragraphs that were almost legible. Inspired by Bud Light commercials, more than one student posed the existential question *Why Ask Why?*

Crossing the faculty parking lot, Win noticed the sun breaking over the rooftops and decided to take a spin up the street to Brewer's Court.

The massive iron gates were wide open. Win's Mustang bowled smoothly over the cobbled courtyard. Constructed of closely-set cream bricks, the towering malt house was fringed with pearl gray scrollwork and Viking gargoyles. Rows of stern, helmeted faces glared fiercely at the blue-overalled construction workers erecting scaffolding against their battlements. Win parked and searched for an entry. A side door was open. Win slipped in and nodded at a contractor, who shifted his cigar and raised a thermos in greeting.

A short flight of stone steps led to the high-ceilinged lobby. The first floor had been leased to a nightclub that promised to be a magnet for upscale female professionals who would be just an elevator ride away. An in-house disco would spare Winfield the need to brave inclement weather, risking icy roads, and potential frostbite. Above all, an elevator eliminated the often tortured "whose car should we take?" debate that ended many a romance in the parking lot.

The second and third levels would house law offices, insurance agencies, investment firms, and brokers. Upper floors that once stored tons of malt were being divided into tri-level condos. Win's unit was on the northeast corner. A rough outline had been spray-painted on the bricked floor. Remembering the designer's blueprints, he took a walking tour through his future home. Chalked lines indicated bathrooms and closets. Other marks represented the Jacuzzi, wet bar, entertainment center, and living room with its sweeping view of Lake Michigan. Upstairs, the loft would contain his study and the master bedroom, both to be equipped with skylights. Win imagined himself cuddling beside a blonde on a waterbed while pondering the night sky. Hooks added to the beamed ceiling would definitely appeal to Barbie.

He took the spiral staircase to the roof. When completed, each unit would have a private roof garden. Walking along the castle-like parapets, Win felt like a prince surveying his realm. No doubt he would have no difficulty coaxing a boozy arbitrageur or two up from the bar on warm summer nights for nude star gazing.

Only one thing tainted his view. Just beyond the brewery gates, stood a squat building of peeling cinder block. Rusted dumpsters, wobbly columns of bald tires, and a dented Volkswagen hood cluttered its small weedy yard. A faded logo was barely visible over dust-streaked windows. KWIK KLEEN.

Win frowned. What an eyesore! The Kwik Kleen chain hadn't operated an outlet in Milwaukee since 1995 when the owner was found in the trunk of his El Dorado in long term parking at O'Hare. He made a mental note to check his plans to see if this parcel of land was slated for renovation.

A few days later at the weekly finance meeting, Win asked one of the contractors if there were any plans to demolish the abandoned cleaners.

"Can't. Don't own the land. See the chart." He tapped a computer generated blueprint with the chewed end of a Churchill reject. A neat semi-circle was cut from the edge of the property line. "Brewery never owned that site. Not in my plans. Check with Jack Lane. He's got all the titles and property records."

Joining Brooks Adams at the refreshment table, Win mentioned the dry cleaners. "I'm wondering what it would cost to buy the lot and demolish the building. It's so old it looks like one good shove would knock it over. We could plant some trees or even put up a sign."

"Good idea, Win. Why don't you handle it?" Sipping decaf, Brooks leaned closer and whispered, "Tell you what, why don't you buy it yourself? See if you can get it cheap. Don't mention us. Maybe some out-of-state outfit owns it and has no idea about the project. You could buy it, clear it, and sell the lot to us at a profit. Hell, we overlooked it, why not make a little killing? That condo down payment is going to be stiff—even with a twenty percent discount."

And he had an extra thousand sitting in his checking account to play with. Win made a few phone calls. A city clerk informed him that the Kwik Kleen property was titled to the owner's widow, Mrs. Vido Spano of Coral Gables, Florida.

"Mrs. Spano?" Winfield telephoned from his Frederick Douglass Savings and Loan office.

"*Si.* Which one? Me or my mother-in-law?"

"Well, I want to talk to the Mrs. Vido Spano who owns a Kwik Kleen building on North Third Street in Milwaukee."

"That's my mother-in-law."

"Is she available?"

"She's in the hospital."

"Oh."

"Had a stroke. She won't be out for a month or two. Can I help? Is this about her taxes?"

There was concern in her voice. "Well," Win began, using the tone he reserved for failing students begging for incompletes, "taxes can pose a serious problem. As well as the potential liability of an abandoned property. Anything can happen. Accidents. Break-ins. Children starting a fire or being injured. Is the property fully insured?"

"Are you an insurance salesman?"

Damn! He'd blown it. Her voice had that "I-saw-something-about-people-like-you-on-*Sixty-Minutes*" edge to it.

"No, this is Doc . . ." he halted. Why use his title and sound like some overpaid MD? People loved soaking physicians with bad investments and stinging them with bum property. "This is Doc Payton. I'm shopping for a site for a donut shop. Like to make an offer on the property."

"Really?"

She seemed thrilled at the prospect. "We tried to sell that store two years ago. Al just got tired of flying back and forth. Say, you know we got a better store with more parking on Capitol Drive. Much better neighborhood."

"How far west?"

"Oh, I can't remember exactly. Ninety-five hundred something."

"Too bad. I already have a store on 92nd Street. But I could use one on Third. I can have my lawyer speak to your husband. I'm a little short of cash, but I think I can scrape up enough to take it off your hands. If it's not too steep," he added cautiously.

"Oh, God. Wait till I tell Al. With all these doctor bills. You wouldn't believe what Medicare don't cover."

"I hope we can work something out."

Win hung up the phone, feeling like Donald Trump at the top of his game. He'd let Brooks and Keisha play with the numbers. If he could get the property for less than seventy-five, he could finance the deal himself without a loan.

Three days later Brooks called with good news.

"Win, guess what? Keisha talked the Spanos into selling for sixty grand."

"Sixty!" Win clenched the phone. "Fantastic."

"We just have to demolish the building and tidy up the site. Let me make a few calls. We could get a minority contractor to do the job. We need the MBE credits. This is going to work out all around. You can probably scoop up a fast twenty percent profit."

Over ten thousand bucks for a few phone calls! Win gazed at his telephone with new respect and began thinking about yet a third career opportunity. No doubt there were other hot properties that could be bought and flipped for a handsome profit. His twentieth reunion was just two-and-a-half years away, and he wanted to make sure he could hold his own with the gynecologists and leverage buyout managers.

"Sounds good, Brooks. Tell Keisha to go ahead. Just let me know what papers she needs from me."

"OK, keep in touch."

As soon as he hung up, Win got a text message from his agent:

> Win,
> Gobel & Gobel dumped your screen treatment. Nix to STREET SISTER. Legal says too close to STREET ANGEL. Will pay $2,000 kill fee.
> Gloria Silverman

Another two grand! Life couldn't get any better. He had totally forgotten about his three-page treatment about a hooker stalking the killer of a teen runaway. It had taken less than an hour to bang out. Jeez, a kill fee a month wouldn't be bad.

While his creative writing class struggled with haiku, Winfield scribbled ideas for bad movies. He tapped his forehead with a number 2 pencil, deep in thought. What would Gobel & Gobel find interesting enough to read and reject with a kill fee but not so interesting to request a complete script? Besides Gobel & Gobel, there were half a dozen other hard R production companies specializing in cable and straight-to-DVD thrillers featuring ex-centerfolds in soft porn tales of serial killers, terrorists, beach detectives, and all-girl biker gangs.

At last he was reaching that precious point when even his bad ideas were worth money. Soon he would be able to collect advances for books unfinished, books unwritten, books unplanned, even book *ideas* doodled on napkins. Agents and editors would carefully fold his Sardi's cocktail napkins, holding them delicately like swatches from the Shroud of Turin. And they would write checks. Big checks.

Win's telephone message light was blinking in C262. There were three messages. Two students explained in rasping voices they had missed the mid-term because of illness. Students always delivered these messages with throaty coughs. On the phone, they believed their ailments had to be audible to be appear genuine. No one called a professor to announce a broken ankle or gall bladder attack in full voice. The final message, from Lionel, was decidedly different. His excited voice boomed loud and clear from the speaker.

"Win, call me as soon as you can! That property you sold us—we struck oil!"

Oil? Win wondered. Oil, in Wisconsin? True, he had recalled reading about Native American tribes protesting drilling, but that was hundreds of miles north, practically in Canada. Win had a spotty knowledge of local history, but to his recollection, no one had ever struck oil in Milwaukee.

Win picked up the phone and rapidly punched out numbers. Lionel's cell phone crackled. He sounded strained and worried. "I'm at the site now. Maybe you should get over here. Brooks is in Chicago and won't get back until six."

Win decided to skip an English Department meeting. Nothing on the agenda concerned him. He did enough for diversity already and would hardly benefit from another ninety minutes of tortured white liberal angst over the Great Ebonics Debate.

Afraid of running into the chairwoman or one of her lackeys in the elevator, Winfield took a utility stairway to the basement garage. Donning sunglasses, he waited for the traffic to clear then rolled out onto Sixth Street, sun visors lowered.

As Win pulled into Brewer's Court, Lionel ran forward arms waving. His lavender jumpsuit, with obligatory pink scarf dangling from his left pocket, was spotless. So much for Win's image of a gusher. Lionel was no James Dean, blackened to the eyes, stumbling from his roadster in *Giant* proclaiming a fountain of instant wealth.

He motioned towards a white step-van parked next to the half-demolished Kwik Kleen building. "I'll let this guy tell you. I didn't do well in chemistry," Lionel explained, tapping at the door.

A grim face appeared at the dusty window. The door opened, and Win followed Lionel inside the truck. There was hardly room to stand in the mobile lab.

"Jack Kleinman, DNR," the glum figure in overalls announced flatly.

Win extended his hand, then withdrew it. Kleinman wore latex gloves and was holding the end of a thin tube as if handling bodily fluids taken from a Bronx junkie.

"This sample should do it. It's from three meters. Just under ten feet. I'm getting clear readings of hydrocarbon presence. You can see the oil sheen."

Leaning closer, Winfield saw a slight shininess to the dark smear on the end of the aluminum probe. A gentle luster, like the patina on three-day-old ham, glimmered in the dim light.

It seemed hardly significant. But then a trace of oil at ten feet might be promising. The gusher might be tapped fifty or a hundred feet lower.

"Mineral rights."

"What?" Lionel asked.

"I think I got the mineral rights," Win said, trying to recall the contract he had signed a few days before. Even if he sold the whole thing to Brewer's Court, it would certainly be worth a bonus.

"What type of oil is it?" Win asked, recalling enough from sophomore earth science to appreciate that oil came in different grades.

"Probably thirty weight with a little ethyl mixed in."

"Ethyl? You mean you hit gasoline?" Didn't gas have to be refined? Could you have a gasoline well?

"It's mixed together in the subsoil of course. God knows how many gallons were spilled over the years."

"Spilled? Where did it come from? It's not natural?"

"In Milwaukee?" Jack Kleinman snorted. "This is no joke. We're not talking about somebody tossing out a dirty oil filter here. Did you notice the islands?"

"Islands?" Win asked.

"Islands. Islands! Those concrete platforms out front," Kleinman barked as if talking to a mental defective. "This was a gas station for fifty years. You didn't know that? The tanks are still underground."

"Oh?" Win asked uncertainly. "How big are they?"

"Probably five thousand gallons."

"You mean they left five thousand gallons of gas down there?" Winfield asked, doing rapid multiplications.

"They may have left a residue of ten or twenty gallons. It's the motor oil that's the real problem."

"Problem?"

"You're looking at major toxic contamination here. You're close enough to the river to face a lawsuit if any of these contaminants entered the runoff."

Win swallowed hard.

"No doubt back then they just dumped used motor oil in a pit in back of the garage. Then there's all those solvents the dry cleaners used. That's another toxic stew."

"What do we do?"

"I just conduct tests. An environmental impact team will have to file a report. I can tell you to get some shovels ready because you're going to have to dig up those tanks and haul them out of here. Then you have to remove all the contaminated soil. This has to be treated and buried."

"What will that cost?"

"Remember that gas station that used to be near the post office downtown?"

"Oh, sure," Win recalled, finally understanding why the entire foundation of the Exxon station had been dug up and removed. It was evidently not, as Winfield previously assumed, an archeological dig.

"Well, that ran half a mil plus fines and land restoration fees."

"Fines?"

"The state levels a fine every day the pollution existed."

"But God, this place was empty for almost twenty years. You can't expect people to pay for that."

"Tell your lawyer. The '93 law has a grandfather clause. Nothing purchased before then could be fined. Only if you bought or sold property without an environmental impact study. Just pull yours and you're covered."

In moments of stress, Winfield turned to his mother. But she was on a Paris buying trip. He left frantic messages at George V, then turned to the next available supportive female. As a criminal defense attorney and wanna-be sex partner, Shelly Bronfman was perfect.

Smoking one Benson and Hedges after another, she tilted her executive chair back and gave Win a sympathetic nod before speaking in her studiedly husky Lauren Bacall voice, "It's clear, Win, you have a problem. Ignorance of the law is no protection."

"But I had a lawyer arrange the deal. She talked to the Spanos. Nobody told me I needed an environmental impact study."

"I know. I know." Leaning forward, she patted his thigh with a heavily-veined, manicured hand. "I know. I know. You've got a problem, but I don't usually handle this kind of thing. Give me a good rape case or a clean shooting where it's one victim's word or a couple of eyewitnesses. People I can tear apart on cross. That's what I do. People say boo about my client, I bust their balls. But you went ahead and signed some papers. Your signature clinches it. Let me call my husband." Her hand slid higher on his inner thigh. "Relax, they found some oil, not a body."

In the days that followed, overalled DNR men trooped through the half-renovated Brewer's Court complex, prying up granite cobblestones, boring holes, and drilling through basement floors to insert probes. Samples were placed in labeled jars and sent to Madison for analysis.

Shortly before Thanksgiving Win received a certified letter instructing him to appear before a hearing. Sidney Bronfman agreed to represent him pro bono. God knows what Shelly had on him.

At the appointed time, a black and gray Rolls Royce swept up to a side entrance of MITI's main building. Winfield climbed into the softly-lit back seat. The car smelled of cologne and cigars. The *New York Times* was strewn across the green carpeted floor. Bronfman, heavyset and scented, sipped coffee from a Wedgwood cup.

"How are ya?" he asked in a whisky-crusted voice. He swelled out his Brooks Brothers suit like a Macy's parade balloon. "Have coffee. It's Colombian. Special blend." He pressed a button with a jeweled finger and a silver carafe rose from a cabinet. Computer screens blinked out commodity prices in neat green numerals.

A smart phone buzzed. Bronfman dug into his expansive vest and retrieved a Samsung in a gold case. "Sidney Bronfman," he announced with quiet importance. He might as well have answered "Henry Kissinger" or "King of England."

Tapping the glass partition, he signaled his Filipino driver on.

Consulting his watch, Bronfman spoke into the phone as if Win were invisible or unconscious. "I dunno, Burt. I got a little legal this morning. A hearing. Handling a little problem for one of Shelly's boys. See you at the club later. And maybe that what's her name can join us. Candy? Chrissy? The blonde." He gave a sexual chuckle then hung up. He, too, placed a veined, manicured hand on Win's thigh, "Don't worry, kid. I'll take care of this. You pay a little fine and walk out the door a wiser man. What the hell, I did it for the Balistrieri's often enough, why not you?"

Throughout the hearing, Bronfman took calls, chatting with clients in Chicago, New York, and the Cayman Islands. The Assistant Southern District Environmental Officer was impressed. A plain, plump blonde in a JC Penney blazer, she smiled nervously, shuffled papers, and haltingly read from state statutes, "Any party possessing property endangering the environment and property of others, whether public or private, with contaminations resulting from the improper disposal of industrial, agricultural, or commercial waste substances shall be liable for a fine of no less than one hundred and no more than ten thousand dollars per day of ownership."

She cleared her throat, then added, "Since you failed to conduct an environmental impact study, you knowingly refused to seek evidence of possible contamination."

Cupping the phone with his soft palm, Bronfman turned and whispered, "My client had no idea the site was contaminated. The previous business was a dry cleaner. How could he know it was a gas station thirty years ago? He ain't clairvoyant. He was only trying to eliminate an eyesore, a liability to the neighborhood. It could have become a crack house. It was urban beautification."

The Assistant Southern District Environmental Officer smiled politely and cleared her throat again. "Despite your well-guided motivations, you did possess the property in question for five full days. You are still liable for any fines incurred. The present owners, Brewer's Court Redevelopment Corporation, will have to restore the site and bear all costs. Given the circumstances, the state feels a fine of five thousand dollars a day would be adequate."

"Hold it, pal," Bronfman whispered to a client calling from Las Vegas. He scowled, then gestured to Win, "This man is providing a community service. He's a teacher. Works in minority business. Inner city redevelopment. He's a man of limited means. Let's not drag this out and go into a full blown hearing or wind up in court. Let's cut to the chase and save the state time and move on. The site will be cleaned up. Why punish my client for being stupid for five days? Look at him, he's naive, a babe in the woods. Pathetic. A guppy swimming with sharks. A grand a day is more than enough."

Glancing at Win like a fourth grade teacher hearing a dog-ate-my-homework story, she nodded pensively. "One thousand dollars a day," she reflected. "I'm sure the Southern District Environmental Office will find that sufficient. Sign here."

Win reached into his pocket for the Mont Blanc he used for signing important documents.

Bronfman kicked him under the table. "Use a Bic," he hissed.

Win let the fountain pen slip back into his pocket and withdrew a plastic Frederick Douglass S&L pen.

"My client will pay in thirty days," Bronfman announced. "Let's go."

In the elevator Bronfman gave him a brief lesson, "When you plead poverty, you don't sign with a five-hundred-dollar fountain pen. And send her a check—certified—today. The full five grand. Don't screw it up." He checked his Rolex. "You don't mind grabbing a cab do you? I gotta catch the interstate for Chicago."

The brass elevator doors slid open. Bronfman, brushed past Win, pinched him, and let out a sexual chuckle, "Keep Shelly happy and outta my hair. *Slan*, Paddy."

The Brewer's Court Redevelopment Corporation's December finance meeting was well attended—despite a blizzard that dumped ten inches of snow the night before. Hampered by the snow and frozen ground, work crews excavating gasoline tanks demanded overtime and hazard pay.

"According to our contractor's estimates, these additional costs should not exceed twenty thousand dollars," Brooks stated hopefully.

The men and women seated around the conference table tapped their copies of the inch-thick report. Accountants threatened to snap pencils. Attorneys who had quit smoking years before patted empty shirt pockets for phantom cigarettes. Everyone anticipated lunch time martinis.

Bundled in parkas and furs, the out-of-state investors were exceedingly glum.

"We should realize that these costs are quite reasonable," Lionel offered. "We have to remove the tanks and dig a hole twenty feet deep to extract all the contaminated soil. The site will be restored. In the spring we can plant a flower bed. This will rectify an environmental problem and enhance the aesthetics of the main entrance."

"At five hundred dollars a daffodil," a banker muttered behind Win.

"Let's not forget the environmental damage we have prevented. This site could have gone undetected for years had this discovery not been made. It could have cost us millions in the future. In a way we are rather fortunate."

Shirley Collingsworth, vice-president of First Chicago Realty, snorted, "I don't call shelling out four-hundred-thousand dollars for a flower bed fortunate." She waved her report. "We get stuck paying four-hundred grand while the prick who sold us this land gets off with a five-thousand-dollar fine! I'll tell you who's lucky! I'd give my last functioning ovary to know just who the fuck this Winfield Payton is!"

Win swallowed hard and snapped his pencil.

HIP-HOP

"Who you wanna be?" the drunken Tin Man challenged, waving a cardboard ax as Winfield entered.

"Wait a minute, sugah. Don't tell me. I know."

Winfield turned to face a mammoth pair of ebony implants swelling over studded leather cups. Good electrolysis job, he noted.

A long, red dagger-edged fingernail traced his cheek.

"Who you wanna-be?" the RuPaul clone asked huskily. "I know, you're Troy Donohue. Anybody tell you you look like Troy Donohue?" she asked, pursing her full red lips.

She leaned closer, "Tell, me baby, what brought you here?"

Winfield was not unaccustomed to being the lone Caucasian in a crowd, and he considered himself gay-friendly. But he was not drunk enough to feel wholly secure as the lone Caucasian heterosexual at The Black Cat's annual costume party. Unmasked, he stood apart from the riot of Beyoncé's clumping past on killer heels. Avoiding eye contact with the leather-strapped gladiators and sword-wielding pirates chugging beer at the pool table, he made his way through the crowd. A pair of Oprahs passed him an oversized brandy snifter bearing party favors—condoms and phallic lollipops.

Winfield slipped a condom in his pocket and went looking for Lionel. Evidently Win was the only one from the S&L to take up his invitation. Making his way between a Don King and an Al Sharpton checking their wigs in a mirror, he headed to the back bar.

Tripping behind him, RuPaul tapped Win on the shoulder, "Listen, baby, who you trying to find?"

"Lionel Adams."

"Mmmmm. Never knew Lionel to have a taste for vanilla, and he does like them taller, but you are cute."

"We work together," Winfield hastily explained.

RuPaul smiled, then leaned forward to press her breasts into Win's face. "Listen, honey," she whispered, "you ever have surgically constructed pussy?"

"Not that I'm aware of," Winfield said tentatively. Did Shelly Bronfman's hysterectomy count?

"I'm built for pleasure," she said, jutting her pelvis forward. "Extra tight, baby. Best ride of your life." She parted the slit in her tight skirt, revealing a smooth hard thigh encased in sheer nylon. "I can crack walnuts between these, honey."

Winfield gulped. "Right," he smiled, gazing frantically for a rescuer.

"Listen, babe. I know what you're thinking. I play safe. Always have. All I want between you and me is latex and a smile."

"Can I get you a drink?" Winfield asked.

"Sure, sugah!"

Winfield bought her a tequila sunrise and a Miller Lite for himself. The Mysterie Ghost Punch was two dollars a mug, but Winfield was in no mood to be adventurous.

He bypassed a trio of suburban gangstas and squeezed behind a black Rhett Butler shouting his phone number to a pair of lumberjacks with pierced ears. The back bar was bedlam. Witches. Hard-hats. Huckleberry Finn and Jim in chaps. Good Witch Glenda tossed glitter over a cluster of black cats of questionable gender. A sweatered Bill Cosby leered, "Hey, hey, hey" while a Naomi Campbell cursed out a Rihanna for copping her lipstick in the men's room.

"That's evil, Miss Thang."

"Who, *moi?*" Rihanna mouthed in exaggerated denial.

Winfield felt a large, strong hand, tipped with inch-long nails, grip his groin.

"Nice package, white boy," a towering Michelle Obama whispered huskily.

"Thanks."

Mike Huckabee should see me now, Winfield thought. God, where was Lionel?

Win edged past a drunken clown clinging to a bar stool. Lionel was nowhere to be seen. Turning to leave, he saw Barbie emerge from the ladies' room wearing a long blonde wig. Silken hair hung to just above her shoulders and swept up to caress her neck. She wore a red bow in her hair, a red and white letter sweater, short red cheerleader skirt, white socks, and tennis shoes.

"Win, what are *you* doing here?"

"Some people from the S&L are supposed to meet after work. I guess I'm the first one."

"Gayle invited me. He came as Tina Turner. And where's your costume? I'm supposed to be Veronica or is she the brunette? You know Archie's girlfriend?"

"Well, you look divine." Winfield was awestruck. Normally, he was accustomed to seeing Barbie nude, in leather, or her Century 21 blazer. Now she looked so young, so virginal, so girlish. Winfield was suddenly drawn back to high school, the year book club, and Sarah Mandel, the ever unobtainable head cheerleader. She was blonde, bosomy, dreamy-eyed, with full lips and a dazzling smile. She was cute and wholesome and hopelessly enslaved to the quarterback.

Barbie moved forward, sipping her Diet Coke. Watching her pink lips purse around the straw, Winfield remembered being sixteen when the most erotic thing in the world was watching Sarah Mandel lick an ice cream cone.

Barbie's eyes flashed with delight. "Win! It's great to see you. You've been so busy we hardly have time to get together. You haven't read any of my emails! I sent you a new version of the cop and hooker. Really hot."

Cop and hooker had been a favorite scenario. But after reenacting the spanking, wrist tying, forced fellatio in her car, his car, the parking structure of the Hyatt, the basement of the Mequon Library, and his laundry room, the routine was getting stale.

As she chatted, he did not listen to her words but studied the movement of her soft pink lips. She looked so young, so fresh. She flicked at her wig like a schoolgirl.

"Why, Win, you're not listening to a word I'm saying," she said, pulling closer.

"Come on," he found himself whispering, "Let's go to my car."

"Fur shure!" She jumped up and down like a kid at Christmas and followed him, her warm hand in his.

A chill winter breeze gently blew Barbie's virginal blonde hair as they strolled down the narrow alley to his car.

"I just love Mustangs," she cooed with girlish delight.

Win opened the door, feeling a pang of latent adolescent lust as she hopped inside. Sliding next to her, he watched her suck a phallic lollipop with pre-puberty innocence.

"You're so beautiful, Barbie."

She turned, wrinkled her nose in Gidget embarrassment and sighed, "Oh, Win, you are so sweet."

He leaned over and softly, briefly kissed her cheek. She purred, gently caressing his neck. Her lips lightly brushed his, sending a thrill to his loins, and more painfully, his heart. "Oh, Win," she sighed.

He stroked her smooth bare thigh. She moaned, moving closer. He cupped her breasts, feeling the erect nipples through her sweater and bra. She sighed deeper, crossing and uncrossing her legs. "Ohhhh, Winnn." Leaning back, she tossed her blonde hair, licked her lips, and moaned. "Oh, yesssss." She moaned louder and squirmed, panting like a Fifties hot chick in a drive-in aflame with Spanish fly. In another minute, she would be humping his gear shift.

He gently but firmly slid his hand higher on her thigh, feeling her shudder with nervous anticipation.

"Oh, Winnn!" she whispered, nibbling on his ear lobe. She squirmed, pressing herself forward, grinding herself against his probing hands. The dampness of her panties excited him. Her hot breath began to fog the windows.

The alley behind The Black Cat was not safe. Police cars regularly prowled the neighborhood, harassing hustlers and transvestite streetwalkers.

"Barbie, let's go to my place."

"Oh, Win, I want it so *baaadd*."

"Come on, it's early," Win urged, wondering why Barbie was hesitating.

Suddenly, she pulled away. "Stop, please stop! Stop!" Tears welled in her eyes. "Oh, Win, I just can't do this. I just can't. I wanted to, but I'm afraid. I just can't. Please, I have to go." She leaned over, kissed him wetly, then grabbed her purse, and bolted from the car. Running to her Volvo, she paused to wipe tears from her eyes.

Win sat helpless and empty as she drove off. He went back inside and ordered a double. The party was revving up, the gays and lesbians and curious straights and horny bi's were in cruise mode, groping and fondling. Shielding themselves behind makeup and masks, they could let their libidos run wild.

Sipping his drink, Win noted the forced gaiety. An immense sadness welled inside him. No doubt in gay bars, dungeons, strip joints, singles bars, massage parlors, and hotel rooms men and women would be playing tonight, their partners, paid or unpaid, masking disgust or faking interest. All over America blind dates were taking place. Contacts made through chat rooms, dating services, singles websites, and personal ads led God knows how many people—at fifteen or fifty—to be nervously gripping a malt or a martini, looking at a door and hoping against all hope to meet someone special. It all seemed so lost, so sordid, and so empty. Whatever happened to love, to genuine passion, to the simple wholesome connection with somebody—sans costumes, hardware, latex, lubricants, and Viagra?

All he wanted was to cuddle up with Barbie forever. But would she leave Jerry? And what about her kids? Suddenly the Brewer's Court condo seemed wildly inappropriate. Children would want a dog and a yard, a swing set, and a neighborhood where they could ride their bikes and sell Girl Scout cookies. If only he had met Barbie when they were both in college. A lifetime of living, sharing, and growing together. The most intense passion was perhaps after all found in conventional, old-fashioned matrimony and not in a chain of costumed play partners.

Lionel was nowhere in sight. Win finished his drink and left the bar. Overhead, dry branches rattled in the breeze. Dead leaves scraped across the broken pavement. Win sighed. His apartment would be empty, lonely. He thought of hitting a few other clubs or making a few last minute calls, but getting drunk or even getting laid would not kill the ache in his heart.

The office provided a refuge of sorts. Work could be distracting. Maybe Ted or Keisha would be working late and they could chat, order a pizza, and pass the night until he was tired enough to sleep.

But Win found himself alone in the century-old building. Sitting at his computer, he wrote and deleted the text of an investor email, watching the words come and go. Giving up, he glanced at the clock and mechanically played solitaire.

His smart-phone vibrated in his pocket.

"Hello?"

"Oh, Win, you were sooo good," Barbie whispered. She let out a stifled sexual chuckle. "You are so inventive. That whole cheerleader virgin scene was so hot. I haven't been so steamed up in a long time. As soon as I got home, Jerry and I fucked our brains out! Win, you are dangerous! You got me so worked up. Listen, I can't talk. I'll send you an email after Jerry falls asleep. Ciao, baby."

GHOST OF THE *RUPTURED DUCK*

"Win, when does your Christmas break start?"

"The nineteenth is my last day of class," Winfield answered, wondering why Brooks bothered to call instead of waiting for their two o'clock meeting.

"Going anywhere?"

"The MLA Convention is in Chicago the first week of January," Winfield said, tapping his MITI desk calendar. "Other than that I will be in town. I've got some writing to do."

Some writing. There were three chapters of his seemingly never-to-be-completed *Critical Thinking for Cultural Diversity: A Workbook* to write. The publisher's deadline had passed. His story about a sudden appointment to a governor's task force on minority student retention had been convincing enough for his editor to grant a sixty-day extension. But even with extra time, it would be tight. He had two hundred pages to grind out.

"I'm open," he found himself saying.

"Feel like a fast trip to Texas?"

Winfield leaned forward, brushing aside a stack of freshman themes. A summons from Brooks was usually lucrative. Income from textbooks, business seminars, and his unsigned club reviews in *Midwest Exotic Dancer* paled before consulting jobs with Frederick Douglass Savings and Loan.

"What have you got?" Winfield asked, his money hunger mounting like junk bond fever.

"I just got off the phone with Bill Reynolds down at Lone Star Savings. Those cowboys are having problems. One default after another. We're going to clean up. They're selling off foreclosed assets for twenty-five cents on the dollar. And Win, you wouldn't believe what they've seized!"

Brooks seemed abnormally excited. "I thought you said we were over-invested in Texas," Winfield reminded him.

"Sure, sure. Who needs another fifty foreclosed ranch houses? There's an office tower outside Houston I want. But the main thing. . . and this is just unreal. . . The main thing is that Lone Star foreclosed the Barr estate. Remember George Barr?"

"The movie actor? The cowboy who made all those spaghetti Westerns?"

"Right. He made a ton of dough in real estate during the bubble. Well, he went bust in 2008 and had to float his empire on loans. He died three years ago, and his son-in-law tried to keep things going. Last week he had to throw in the towel, and Lone Star foreclosed. They grabbed all kinds of property and movie stuff. You will never believe what's on the block. And nobody knows about it yet. Just us. They have a B-25 mothballed in a hangar outside Houston."

"A B-25? You mean a bomber?"

"B series. The same model used in the Doolittle raid. It's mint. Completely restored for a movie project that fell through."

"An airplane?" Win asked again, still not sure he was following Brooks.

"Sure. Do you know what a collector would pay for something like that? The Lone Star guy had me drooling. The ship probably just needs a good overhaul and an FAA check. Once we get the papers and insurance in order, we can fly her home."

"A B-25? You mean like the plane on display at Mitchell Field?"

"Sure. Just a different model. The thing is this, can you fly down Friday and check it out? I'll be stuck in town until the fifteenth. Besides, it's a chiclet run. Reynolds sounds as prejudiced as hell. You'll probably run into the son-in-law. He's still tight with Lone Star. George Barr was a right wing nut. I don't imagine the family would want to see one of their toys sold to a black guy. Bijan has his multi-engine license, but they probably won't cotton to an Iranian either. I'd appreciate it if you could go down and check the plane out and make an offer."

"How much?"

"Lone Star wants cash. If we can offer 150 G's, they might just take it. That's what the army paid for those birds back in '42. Just by the inflation factor, the plane's worth a million and a half. Maybe more. How many B-25's can there be left?"

"What are you going to do a bomber?"

"Fly it! Air shows. Fourth of July celebrations. Think of the publicity! It will get us in tight with veterans, the kinds of folks who'd never think of doing business with a black outfit. Besides, it's a public service. This is a piece of history."

Brooks' enthusiasm was infectious. Pushing forty, having avoided Iraq, Haiti, Bosnia, and Afghanistan, Win harbored a non-combatant's guilt about his secret fascination with WWII. Browsing in Barnes & Noble, he was inevitably lured to the oversized discount editions of *Planes of the Third Reich* or *Destination Normandy*. His pacifist heart began to beat like a tom-tom.

"When can you get over here?"

"My last class ends at one."

"Great. I'll send Lionel to get some books from the library. See you then, boyo."

The subzero afternoon was blinding. The sun blazed in a cloudless arctic blue sky. Glazed in snow and ice, the neo-classic S&L shimmered like a frosted wedding cake. In the brilliant domed lobby, the commanding oil portrait of Frederick Douglass seemed less grim in the snow-reflected light. There was even a hint of a smile in the old boy.

Brooks and Lionel were circling the conference table when Winfield arrived.

"Win! Great to see you. Check out the books Lionel picked up. Here's a diagram. The B-25. One of the greatest planes of World War II. Twin Wright engines. Seventeen-hundred horsepower. Two-hundred-and-eighty-five miles an hour max speed. That's power! We could make the East Coast in four hours. God, we have to get this."

Winfield flipped through the books spread across the oak table. Exploded diagrams showed details of the cockpit, machine gun turret, and bomb bay. War movies came back to him. Spencer Tracy lifting off the deck of the *Hornet* in *Thirty Seconds Over Tokyo*.

"Isn't she grand?" Brooks asked. "One of the best planes they ever built. Look at that tail configuration. First class. Here's the thing, Win. We've got to be sharp. I want you to check out an office building as a ruse. Spend a lot of time and ask a lot of questions. Take notes and shoot some videos. Keep them talking and make a lot of calls to us. Just chat with Joyce or Lionel. We have to make them think we want to make an offer on the building. Then, mention the plane. Say you know some retired Air Force colonel who might make an offer if the price is right. Act like it's a favor, your own deal on the side. Say you're willing to put down a few thousand just to hold it. Check out the plane and take pictures. Make sure to get shots of the engines. I'll go over the plans with you and make a list of things to look for."

"Who's going to pay for this?"

"We'll use discretionary funds. I'll finance it myself if I have to. My old man will kick something in, too. He'll be thrilled. He flew a two-engine prop in Nigeria in the Eighties. I'll pay you five thousand plus expenses if you can nail this down." He slapped Win on the back, "Isn't this wild?"

The following day, Winfield gave his composition classes an unannounced in-class writing so he could concentrate on memorizing specifications of the B-25. As he studied diagrams of wings, cowlings, and wheel assemblies, his anticipation mounted. After class, he drove to the Burlington Coat Factory and bought an official replica bomber jacket made in Taiwan.

The executives of Lone Star Savings and Loan greeted Winfield at the Houston airport like an arriving sheik. He could see the hunger in their eyes. Taken to lunch by Chris Bellows, a vice-president, Winfield noted his relief when he refused a drink offer and ordered the house salad.

Munching the special-of-the-day tuna melt, Bellows tapped Winfield's business card. "Frederick Douglass," he drawled. "I heard of a Frederick Douglass back in school. Was he that..."

"He invented the linotype machine," Win answered, self-consciously smoothing his blond hair.

"Oh."

As instructed, Winfield spent most of the day walking through an empty office tower, making notes and asking questions about square footage, sprinkler and alarm systems, signage, insurance premiums, and taxes. From time to time he made phone calls, holding enthusiastic conversations with his voicemail. As they drove to the savings and loan, Winfield ventured, "Chris, going over your list of assets, I noticed you have the Barr estate. There's some sort of plane for sale?" he asked offhandedly.

"The army plane? Yep, that's been stored in a private hangar."

"I suppose it's just scrap now," Win mused, gazing out the window.

"Oh, no, it's all sealed up in plastic. Barr was real particular about it. His uncle flew one in the war. Shot down over Italy, I think."

"You know," Win hinted, hoping to not to sound too interested, "There's a guy I know in the Shamrock Club who's into old planes. Retired Air Force colonel. He still flies. Goes to all the air shows. He might be interested if the price isn't too steep."

"Well, it's not just a matter of price, but of time. We have to move on this property. We have an audit coming up, and we need cash."

"I could put down a deposit, just until I talk to the guy. If I know him, he'll pay cash. He hates loans. He sold his tavern last year, so he should be good for it. But, I'll have to talk him. . ."

"What could you put down?"

"Five thousand."

"Deal." Chris Bellows nodded. Dollar signs danced in his eyes. Smiling, he pulled into a Taco Bell and even offered to buy Win a burrito supreme. "I'll talk to Bill as soon as we get to the office. Jack Hughes, that's Barr's son-in-law, would be glad to tell you about the plane. He's trying to sell his Cessna."

Winfield hid his smile by crunching into a cardboard taco.

The next morning Winfield met Jack Hughes in the flickering neon lobby of the Rialto Cinema.

"I've been able to hang onto the theaters," Hughes said. "We're one of the last independent chains around. We've got sixteen screens in Texas and New Mexico," he said, gesturing with smooth white hands. He was cowboy lean and muscular but pale. A modern Texan, he kept in shape by pumping iron in air-conditioned spas, swimming in indoor pools, and avoiding the carcinogenic sunshine. Pushing through a revolving door, he paused to don a cap and dark glasses before heading outside. Guiding Win to his BMW, he turned to point to the marquee. "The old man used to show his flicks here for his cronies. Served shrimp in popcorn boxes and Jack Daniels in Dixie cups. Quite a character. Drunk, he was a sonofabitch. Sober, he had real class. I hear you wanna see the *Ruptured Duck*?"

"The what?"

"The old army crate, the B-25. Don't know why anyone would want that. Expensive as hell to maintain. And the ride. Christ, it's like a dump truck on a dirt road. It's not pressurized. You bake on the runway and freeze at eight thousand feet. The Cessna's a better deal. Padded seats, bar, computers, DVD player. I'll let it go for one-twenty. Engines have less than three hundred hours."

"Well, I don't fly. But I have a friend who just might want the bomber. Retired Air Force."

"Well, that's Bill Reynold's problem, not mine. I'm no dummy. The stuff I wanted didn't get tagged for collateral. The old man had a '37 Packard and a '41 Caddy. Cherry. I'm keeping the Caddy. The Packard and the Cessna will be enough to bail me out and pay my kid's tuition. I might even ditch the theaters if I get a chance. I never liked running movie houses. The ushers steal you blind. But the old man loved them. They were his last link to Hollywood. Gave him a reason to call the studios once a month and act like a player. Hell, I'd rather go back to teaching fifth grade. Spend my summers in France. But, I'll show you the plane. Chris has the keys to the padlocks. He should be there by the time we arrive. Promise me, though, let me take you up in the Cessna. Just a test flight. Your Air Force pal might have a friend."

"Oh sure, love to," Win promised.

Unlocking the hangar, Chris Bellows snapped on the lights.

"Wow!" Winfield exclaimed, immediately cursing himself for dropping out of character.

"Yeah, right out of *Citizen Kane*. Old man Barr sure loved to collect stuff and could never throw anything away. Movie props. Boats. Cars. Airplane engines. The front porch off a cowboy saloon. Saddles. The plane's in back."

Draped in plastic, the bomber resembled a giant cocooned insect.

"It's pretty dirty. You might want to change. We have overalls in the office."

"Good idea," Winfield said in a bored tone. "I don't want to ruin a good suit on the off chance some washed up pilot might buy a surplus crate."

While Win changed, Jack Hughes and Chris Bellows pulled back the plastic sheathing gone opaque with dust.

"There's a story to this plane," Hughes said. "It never left the States. After the Doolittle Raid, the army painted up some ships for a bond tour. It was loaned out to a movie studio. In '46 it went to an Air National Guard unit. Then the old man bought it for hunting trips. He had it fully restored in '93. Spent half a million hoping to nail down a movie deal. He bought a script about a bunch of WWII vets who fix up a bomber for a war movie then use the plane to smuggle pot in from Mexico. He had Ernest Borgnine and Bob Stack in mind for the leads. But the drug angle scared off his producers, so the idea was scrapped. Listen, Chris and I have to get back to town. Suppose we pick you up in a couple of hours?"

"Sure. Take your time."

Alone with the *Ruptured Duck*, Winfield opened the forward hatch and climbed the small ladder. The interior smelled of dust and metal. Trying to stand, he bumped his head. The pilots' compartment was smaller than the front seat of his Mustang. Having pored over online diagrams and coffee-stained army air corps manuals, he knew what to look for. He crawled into the greenhouse of the nose then slid down the narrow tunnel over the bomb bay leading to the gun turret and tail. His initial curiosity satisfied, he clambered out and set to work. He rigged up some work lights and started taking videos.

Leaning forward in his executive chair, Brooks Adams gripped the Naugahide armrests with nervous excitement as he watched his laptop.

"You can see the interior has been completely restored to the original specifications. Even the fire extinguishers are authentic," Winfield explained. "I found the machine guns and some empty ammo cans."

"OK, OK, I don't have to see anymore. He took the deposit, right? Call Bellows back. You talk to him, I'm too excited."

An hour later, Winfield told Brooks to check his email.

"Did we get it?"

"Take a look. He went for the hundred and fifty grand less the deposit. I told them the check's on the way."

"I'm sending Larry Gates down this weekend. He's the best aviation mechanic I know. He works on his uncle's DC-3. He'll check out the engines and tell us what we need to get her airworthy. God, Win, this spring we can fly her to the Coast!"

Christmas was always a special time for Winfield. After the rush of final exams and the first blasts of Wisconsin's blizzards, he flew home to the comparative warmth of New Jersey. Pushing forty and single, he could bask in the extended adolescence of being an only child home from college. Christmas vacation meant Broadway shows, dinners at Sardi's, nights in Atlantic City, the candlelit service on Christmas Eve, presents, visits from relatives, shopping sprees, and boozy rendezvous with ex-girlfriends now divorced and restless. In his old room, Winfield pored over his high school yearbook and called his very first girlfriend, recently separated from her third husband. She was eager to talk. She was writing a book in hopes of making an appearance on *The View* and wanted advice. She had four chapters written and a prospective title—*Sex in My City*.

Just after Christmas each year, the Modern Language Association convenes for a three-day convention. English professors, grammarians, Italian linguists, Marxist critics, Shakespearean scholars, feminist rhetoricians, gay poets, e-novelists, film makers, tenured entrepreneurs, editors, jobless PhD's, failed playwrights, rising essayists, deconstructionist hacks, Melville biographers, Kerouac bloggers, haiku Tweeters, and wanna-be Angelous converge in hotel lobbies, crowding the bars and lounges between seminars. Hundreds come to present papers. Thousands come to find jobs, hawk books, get published, or get laid. The event is part Super Bowl, part slave market, part fashion show. An ego carnival. A place to be seen and quoted. Attendees wear preppie tweeds and khaki slacks, Armani silks, Greenpeace plaid, Castro fatigues, and Sears interview suits. Women either shroud themselves in earth-toned ponchos or squeeze into leather skirts so taut they can't sit down. Leaning against pillars for support, they debate doctrinal points with tattooed lesbians.

In the arena of oppressed-women-of-color-resisting-cultural-genocide, white males are not marketable commodities. Seeking refuge among the oppressed, Winfield Payton took heart in his Irish roots and put an IRA button on his lapel just as the plane touched down at O'Hare. Anything to escape the generic white man stigma. No WASP he. BRITS OUT!

The convention air was electric with the power of ten thousand horny egos revving at fever pitch. Every statement casually tossed out in a crowded Hyatt elevator had been rehearsed to be memorable. Everyone in his or her own mind was a star, a celebrity, the next Susan Sontag, the next John Simon. And like the defense contractors and stockbrokers they despised, they were driven by money. In seventy-two hours, millions of dollars in salaries, publishing contracts, lecture fees, and research grants would be awarded over vegetarian brunches.

Normally, teaching in a two-year vocational school would earn Winfield the credibility of a disbarred chiropractor crashing an AMA banquet. But the fact that MITI served nine thousand African-American students gave him a platform. White liberals and black conservatives attended his presentation on Black English. It was a carefully crafted paper—designed to offend no one and justify his expense account. He gave his talk, answered questions for fifteen minutes, then excused himself to get where the real action was.

The exhibition hall was jammed. Two hundred publishers displayed books and solicited manuscripts. It was a literary stock market open three short days a year. Walking onto the killing floor, Winfield went into his trader mode. Fueling himself on coffee, Diet Coke, and Ballygowan, he button-holed acquisition editors from McGraw Hill, Prentice-Hall, and Weidenfield & Nicholson. Thinking fast, he made up book proposals on the spot—multicultural anthologies, Islamic readers, politically correct and politically challenging work books. Christian rhetorics. Cold war novels. Third World novels. A rain forest novel. A novel about the Bay of Pigs invasion, half in Spanish. A cycle of poems based on the latest LA riots. A stream-of-consciousness first-person novel about a Hispanic transsexual called *Between Worlds*. A Yeats biography. A Brendan Behan bibliography. Spitting out ideas faster than he could remember them, he bugged himself with his voice recorder and scribbled hieroglyphic notes the back of ATM slips. He collected business cards, dispensed business cards, gulped Jameson from a Boku box, and pressed on like a Kirby vacuum cleaner salesman facing eviction.

Back at his hotel, fueled on hot coffee and ice-cold Diet Coke, he pounded his laptop, generating impressive, though admittedly sketchy, book proposals, trying desperately to remember the ideas that stormed through his mind while chatting up editors. Fearful his emails would be deleted unread, he raced to Kinko's and printed copies to be casually delivered the next morning, "Hi, remember we talked yesterday about a book, well, I just put together a few ideas." Like a cheating lover, he tried to convey the impression he was courting a single editor.

On the second day Barbie called. Win grabbed his smart phone. Twinges of carpal tunnel were shooting through his strained wrists. Laptop keyboards were always a pain to work on.

"We're visiting my sister-in-law in Winnetka," she whispered. "I can get away for two hours. I'll meet you at the Palmer House for a drink. Seven sharp."

Unlike the shivering tourists from LA and Miami who bundled into cabs for a two-block trip, Barbie and Winfield leisurely strolled the subzero streets. Michigan Avenue was ablaze with holiday decorations. Passing the Christmas wreaths, shimmering electric candles, and smiling Santas, Winfield felt a lonely tug of nostalgia, a wistful remorse for lost innocence and lost love. Gripping Barbie's arm, he escorted her through the Hyatt lobby into the glass elevator that whisked them high above the boozy conventioneers reeling from a cash bar sponsored by the Virginia Woolf Society.

Once inside his room, Barbie slipped off her leather trench coat. She seemed so young, so soft, so desirable in her white turtleneck and black ski slacks. A rosy cheeked sophomore gliding off the slopes for hot chocolate. Winfield reached into his pocket and handed her a small box.

"Just a little something for Christmas."

Lifting the gold chain from the red felt-lined case, she pursed her lips, "This is not necessary."

"It's just a gift," Winfield said, moving forward to kiss her.

Pulling back, Barbie raised a warning finger. "Look, we don't have that kind of relationship. I don't *cheat* on my husband, OK? That's not what this is about. You know that. What we have, well, it's different. It's *not* personal."

"Well, I just thought a little something for Christmas," Winfield explained, his memories of college ski dates and hot chocolate fading.

"Look, I have only an hour," Barbie said matter-of-factly. She peeled off her clothes like someone diving into a river to save a drowning child. Clad in black bra and garter belt, she reached into the pockets of her trench coat and pulled out a pair of leather cuffs and a short strap.

"This is all I could bring. Do you have anything?"

Winfield sadly shook his head.

Pouting, Barbie opened the closet and removed Winfield's spare belt. She tested it against her bare thigh. "OK," she muttered, "this will have to do."

She motioned Winfield to follow her into the bathroom. Facing the bathtub, she reached up to grip the shower rod. "I'm ready," she whispered, guiding Winfield's hand to her tight, waiting buttocks.

Back at home, Winfield kept busy with committee work, plans for the spring semester, and the ninth draft of a screenplay his agent patiently reminded him had been rejected twenty-seven times. Brooks kept in touch, calling from Texas and emailing pictures.

"We've rented a hangar. Larry's running compression tests. We need new tires. New plugs. I'm writing checks like crazy. We'll test the right engine next week. I'm going to do a little bargain-hunting while Larry works on the plane. We found a guy living at the VA who used to work on B-25's. He's a Section Eight, but he knows planes."

Winfield was revising a syllabus when Brooks called from Houston.

"Win, we've got our FAA papers in shape and the insurance nailed down. It's going to cost an arm and a leg. But the Duck is ready to fly. Get down here by Tuesday, and you can make our first long-run flight."

"What do you think?" Brooks asked a week later as a small tractor pulled the B-25 from the hangar.

"I feel like a Hollywood extra," Winfield said, no longer self-conscious in his scarf and bomber jacket.

Its wartime markings blazing against the olive drab fuselage, the *Ruptured Duck* stood poised on the concrete apron, full of deadly power. New aluminum props gleamed in the Texas sun.

"Wait till you get inside. We spent a week dusting and scrubbing. Larry brought everything up to spec."

Winfield gazed up at the plane, remembering the first time he hefted the .45 his uncle brought back from Viet Nam. Raw masculinity was facing his student-deferment soul. He had grown up in the shadow of weapons and the men who handled them. Sherman tanks. PT boats. Hellcats and P-38's. Subs and destroyers. M-1's and satchel charges. Moving closer, he studied the daffy, cross-eyed duck painted on the nose. Men in his grandfather's generation had died in planes like this. America, at the height of her power, carpet-bombed the cities of the world with planes like this. For Winfield this was a moment of sociopolitical epiphany.

"Ready for takeoff? Larry's going to be our co-pilot and navigator. You can be the observer," Brooks said, like a coach assigning outfield positions. "Take the bombardier's slot. You ought to get some great shots from the nose. Well, let's move." Brooks drew Larry and Winfield together in a huddle and shook their hands as if making a solemn pact. Reaching up, they patted the fuselage for luck then climbed aboard.

Brooks belted himself in the pilot's seat, donned headphones, and tugged his silk scarf, "I feel just like Van Johnson." He shrugged, then smiled, "Well, maybe Denzel Washington. OK, strap yourself in, guys. And wherever you go, put on a headset so we can communicate. We'll never be able to talk above the engines. OK, ready on the right?"

"Check," Larry said, studying the instruments.

The engine pinged, coughed, then like some monstrous lawn mower, rumbled to life, shaking the plane with a deafening roar. Peering out the navigator's window, Win watched the blades flash silver before becoming a translucent disc.

"Ready on the left?"

"Check."

Both engines thundering, the throbbing bomber pulled forward, the nose wheel bouncing.

Win clutched his seat with trembling arms. The plane taxied, paused for clearance, then rolled forward, engines drumming. Win felt the plane bounce once, then peel upward. Swallowing hard, he unbuckled his seat belt and carefully crawled to the nose.

Seeing the trees sweeping beneath him, Winfield's stomach clenched. Roads, cars, a stretch of freeway, ranch houses, and strip malls raced under him. Brooks broke left, the plane veering on a forty-five-degree angle. Remembering the headphones, Win scrambled to put them on. He picked up the interphone and shouted, "Brooks, where are we going?"

"Over the Gulf. I want to try some low-level stuff."

Watching the Texas scrubland rush under the nose, Win leaned against the throbbing metal shell, savoring the moment. How many men had experienced this, the long flight into harm's way? The dry land beneath them could have been North Africa, war-torn Italy, Iraq. How naked crewmen must have felt in this bay window facing a sky full of fighters. How many men had died in this spot, ripped apart in a shower of machine gun bullets and shattered Plexiglas?

"Getting some good shots?" Brooks' voice crackled in the headphones.

"Yes," Winfield answered, fumbling with the interphone.

"See that refinery just ahead? Focus on that. We're going to make a bombing run."

The *Ruptured Duck* veered to the right then dove hard, engines screaming. The ground raced up, the trees mushrooming upward. Win gasped, pulling back from the nose as if the thin metal hull would protect him in a crash. He aimed his phone, trying to steady himself in a yoga position. As the plane tore across the Texas scrubland at 300 mph, Brooks' voice came over the headphones, singing, "*I don't want to set the wo-orld on fi-uh, just To-ke-o!*"

The plane leveled off at five hundred feet, the refinery tanks sweeping into view.

"Bomb bay doors open."

Win heard the whine of a small motor as he tightened his legs around the bombsight.

"We should have brought water balloons!"

The refinery shot past and the plane rose, streaking toward the clouds.

"Win," Brooks' voice crackled in the headphones, "crawl back to the turret and take some shots of the tail."

"Roger."

Win made his way through the narrow tunnel, feeling the throbbing motors vibrate throughout his body.

In the turret, he plugged in his headphones and aimed his smart phone at the tail, watching the twin rudders turn in lazy unison. He switched the turret on and rotated, the machine guns swiveling against the wind.

Swooping over the shoreline, the B-25 raced over the Gulf, low enough for Win to look up and see the masts of sailboats flash by. Brooks shouted through the interphone,

"This is great! Flat out at forty feet! Win, you have got to get your multi-engine license."

"Watch it Brooks," Larry warned. "Those props need clearance. One high wave and we'll be swimming home."

"OK, gang," Brooks warned, "grab hold because we're hunting for heaven."

Win was pitched forward. Glancing down the tail, he could see the shimmering waves as the plane tilted up, engines racing. Slipping from the turret, Win scrambled forward on hands and knees as if climbing a sliding board. As he reached the navigator's well, he heard Larry shouting.

"Brooks! Ease off, man! Ease off! Check your instruments! The left engine is heating up."

Brooks throttled back and leveled the plane.

"What is it?" Win shouted.

"Nothing serious, I hope," Brooks shouted over his shoulder. "Must be an oil leak in the left engine. She's running hot."

"I should have never let that goddam psycho touch those fittings," Larry cursed.

"Is it bad?" Winfield asked.

"We have to put down fast unless we want ten thousand in repairs."

"Win," Brooks called out, "check the maps. I want to bring her in. Damn these instruments. Christ, what I'd give for digital read outs."

Glad to be of use, Win spread the maps over the small navigator's shelf. "Where are we?" he asked Larry.

"Nearest landfall is San Leon, dead ahead. Three minutes away."

"OK, OK, there's Galveston!" Win shouted into the interphone.

"No good, no good," cried Brooks. "Too far. Look for something closer. Any place. We have to land."

"Brooks, the FAA won't like a forced landing. There will be an investigation," Larry warned.

"Hell, look at this engine! We're going to lose her if we keep going, and I don't want to feather it and try to land on one prop. Win, check out the bottom of the engine. Tell me what you see!"

Win scrambled under the flight deck to the Plexiglas nose, banging his knee on a support. Craning his neck, he pressed his face against the cold clear plastic and saw thick ribbons of oil streaming from the engine, lacing the wing like chocolate swirls on a sundae.

He grabbed the interphone. "It's leaking oil all over," he shouted, wishing he could be more precise. How much oil did the engine contain, five quarts, fifty gallons?

"OK, get up here and help with the maps."

At the navigator's shelf, Win studied the Exxon map of south Texas.

"How about a stretch of road?" he suggested.

"Great, find me one without any traffic or telephone poles on the shoulders. We have sixty-seven feet of wingspan to put down."

Sweeping low over the beach, the plane lumbered on as Win searched the map.

"What's this green up ahead, on the left? Looks open."

"Golf course," Win said, noting the map's miniature ball and flag stick.

"Great. Anything but scrub and sand. Give me some nice firm turf. We set down on sand, and we'll nose over for sure. A hard packed beach is OK, but, Christ, if the tide comes in, we could lose the ship."

"Go for the golf course," Larry cautioned. "Just watch you don't snap off the nose wheel. Don't even think about making a three point."

The B-25 circled the lush manicured lawns. Men and women in white pants and skirts emerged from under candy-striped umbrellas. The club house emptied. Sunburnt salesmen put down their Manhattans and waved.

"See that strip up ahead, looks flat and open," Larry pointed. "Drag the field and check the trees for wind direction."

"Here we go!" Brooks cried as the plane slowed and gently sank between the trees, touching down just past the ninth hole. Win felt two hard bounces, then the ship rumbled over the grass, the thick turf gently gripping the tires.

"Switches off!"

"Switches off!" Larry repeated.

Stillness. Silence. Winfield's ears still rang. The voices coming from the cockpit sounded hollow and distant.

"Let's check the landing gear," Brooks said, unsnapping his seat belt.

Dropping from the hatch, Winfield spotted a pair of golf carts humming toward the plane. Dressed in carefully pressed white Sansabelts and matching red shirts, the Japanese executives stared at Win, murmuring to each other with tight, grim lips. The unspeakable, the obscene had landed in their midst.

Brooks tucked his silk scarf out of view. Larry self-consciously kicked a tire, avoiding their eyes. Win crossed his arms to hide the bomber insignia stitched on his jacket.

A third golf cart raced through the trees. The driver, red-faced and pudgy, gave up. Jumping from his cart, he knocked Miller Lite cans and French fries to the ground. In his white shoes, red pants, and large-bellied alligator shirt, he resembled an irate Buddy Hackett. Win strolled calmly toward him. No doubt this sixty-five-year-old would appreciate this token of his youth, this testament of his country's glory days. Smoothing his blond hair, Winfield stepped forward and extended his hand, flashing a Kiwanis smile.

Standing next to the disdainful Japanese, the man brandished his nine iron like a shillelagh and shrieked, "Do you fucking idiots know how much these fucking greens fucking cost?"

A SIP OF AMONTILLADO

"For the love of God, Montresor!"

"Now, when we come to the work of Arthur Miller, a dramatist our male editor deems significant enough to include *two* of his plays in our anthology, we see a very dissimilar case." Andrea Kaufmann, Ph.D. candidate, paused to catch her breath, then continued. "We see the work of a neo-reactionary sexist. What more could we expect from a writer who sought fame in Hollywood—both these plays were made into movies remember—and the body of its leading sex victim Marilyn Monroe? Would we respect David Mamet if he wrote *Iron Man* scripts and married Miley Cyrus?"

No one in the surgical white seminar room dared object or appear bored. Her aviator glasses flashing in the fluorescent light, Angela tapped her laptop. "It is very obvious that in *All My Sons* Miller is not attacking the military industrial complex at all. No, the play merely demonstrates a conflict between father and son. The war veteran Chris with all his Rambo macho love for his fallen buddies vs. the corruption of a petty businessman trying to protect his loot. Miller never addresses the causes of war, never attacks capitalism. I see nothing redeeming in this work at all, certainly not for women or people of color. I don't see how anyone can see anything in this play or *Death of a Salesman*, for that matter. All of Miller's females are weak, superstitious characters who throw their lives away on dead sons or deadbeat husbands."

"Do you agree, Dr. Payton?" someone asked.

What? Winfield looked up from his legal pad. Had someone asked him a question? Was Andrea done already? Revising a sales brochure extolling the virtues of distressed debt, he hadn't been listening for the last fifteen minutes.

"Well, I think Ms. Kaufmann has given us a great deal to consider. Our time is just about up, and I suggest that next Wednesday we open with this point." A footnote in a foreword came to mind, rescuing him. "When *All My Sons* opened in the Soviet Union, the critics were very harsh. In their view, Chris' shock at his father's deception suggested that honesty was the capitalistic norm. Clearly in their view, Joe Keller's actions were to be perceived as typical capitalistic machinations, not ethical deviations. See you next week."

Winfield gathered his papers, stuffed them into his briefcase, and headed for the nearest stairwell. Elevators were too risky. Waiting for the doors to open, he was an easy target for students wanting help with a research paper or advice on a resume. He jogged down the steps, hoping he would not run into anyone he knew. An extra eight hundred dollars a month was not worth all this. Next semester I'll quit, he promised. Putting up with graduate students was hardly compensated by the ego stroke of teaching in a "real university" instead of MITI, which paid better anyway.

Carefully belted into his Mustang, he pulled out of the guest faculty parking lot and headed downtown. Win slid in a Sinatra CD and mentally shifted gears. Out of academia. Into business. Into two-hundred-dollar an hour consulting. Into the S&L. Into PR. Into "let's grow our way of poverty." Into dreams. "We have a dream" had been his best slogan for Frederick Douglass Savings and Loan. It was emblazoned across full page ads in community newspapers, theater programs, billboards, and complimentary golf pencils distributed at Twin Oaks, that staunchly black and very Republican country club.

He was about to pick up his phone, when something flashed in the rear view mirror. A Jaguar, fire-red, was closing fast. Like an Exocet missile, it tore up behind him, then passed by, horn blaring. Forced onto the shoulder, Winfield banged his steering wheel.

Sonofabitch!

Win pulled back into traffic and zipped into the fast lane, dodging semis. The red Jag weaved a quarter mile ahead, slipping in and out among the housewife-going-to-pick-up-the-kids-SUV's, battered Hispanic Camaros, Shiite Novas, NRA pickups, and patriotic Buicks.

Damn!

Win floored it, tearing up the pitted concrete. But it was too late. The red car was gone. Where are the speed cops when you need them? He turned up Sinatra and patiently threaded his way through traffic. An overturned municipal truck had spilled a ton or more of biodegradable yard waste over two lanes. Win followed a school bus, kid faces leering at him behind smudged windows. Sinatra was crooning about autumn in New York. It didn't help.

Turn signal on, Winfield decided to abandon the billion-dollar expressway system for potholed city streets. Despite the intersections, the stop signs, the double-parked delivery vans, Michigan Avenue would be faster. He was edging toward the exit ramp when the red Jag appeared again, screaming around the pile of would-be compost, beating him to the exit and forcing him behind the school bus.

Damn!

Win pounded the steering wheel. The kids in the bus smirked, twisting their faces with dirty fingers. As the Jag peeled up the ramp, Win caught the license plate. FTJ-654. He jotted it down on the back of a parking ticket. FTJ-654. Repeating the letter-number combination to himself, he smiled. OK, Fortunato.

The incident left Winfield shaken. Reduced to impotent rage, his legs trembled. What would have happened had he caught up with the Jag? Win was ill-equipped for physical confrontation. Despite his workouts, his power lifting, his diet, he was still five-six and needed two hands to fire a .45 with accuracy. A train of feminist significant others had sapped his manhood, softened his edge, tamed his killer instinct.

"Win, what's wrong? You OK?" Lionel asked as Winfield stormed past the receptionist's counter.
"Nothing important. Just some nut on the freeway. Tried to run me off the road."
"Too bad. You ready for the meeting?"
"Sure." Winfield watched Lionel adjust his George Will bow tie and brush his carefully styled hair. Nothing, not war, riot, not even a personal denunciation from Jessie Jackson could shake Lionel's conservative soul. Win felt shamed. He immediately dismissed fire-bombing the Jaguar as an unconscionable act for a college educated Presbyterian. Besides, he might get caught.

During the meeting, Win took notes, made suggestions, and as usual volunteered to create all the media needed to secure board approval for a three-million-dollar investment in African cocoa futures. But his Irish, though not up, smoldered.

Afterwards, he stopped in Ted Kaleem's office. The former FBI man was Kojak tough, blooded in undercover work. But how to ask? Would it be unseemly for a white guy to bring Ted his dirty work, to assume that he freelanced as muscle?

Ted glanced up from his desk.

"Can I help you, Win?"

"Well, uh, yes. There is something. A question. One of my students had her car banged up in the parking lot. She got the plate number, but thinks she transposed the numbers. She wants to check."

"Wisconsin tag?"

"Uh, yes."

"No problem. Got the number?"

"Sure."

Ted pointed to the computer. "We're online with DMV for car insurance. Stop by anytime or have Jessica take care of it."

The cocktail hour at Twin Oaks was in full swing. Gold-braided white undergraduate waiters darted among the middle-aged black men sporting flag pins on their lapels. Rudy Smith, Jackson State '69, was shaking hands and collecting checks for his reelection campaign. Representing Frederick Douglass Savings and Loan, Winfield simply smiled and waved. The cash donation, a Marshall Field's shopping bag stuffed with untraceable tens and twenties, had already been delivered.

Rudy leaned forward and grabbed Win's hand, jerking his arm like a pump handle. "I knew you guys would come through for me." Drawing closer, he whispered, "We have to keep those . . . . liberals in Madison on the run before they get us all on food stamps." For Win's benefit, Smith deleted "white" from "liberal." Smiling, Rudy pressed a gold elephant key chain into Win's palm.

At the bar Win ordered a Diet Coke.

"What are you doing here, Dr. Payton?"

Win recognized the bartender as a former student from his TA days.

"Representing some clients." Always eager to impress those who remembered him from his impoverished grad school years, Winfield was about to spill out a train of success stories. His days as a VW-driving teaching assistant were over, and he wanted the world to know it.

A voice booming from behind caught his attention. Win turned. At six-six, Gayton Phillips dominated the room. Despite gray hair, professorial beard, and Italian suit, he looked like a linebacker ready for scrimmage.

"So this punk tears into the lot and almost smashes my car and gives me the finger. Hell, I pulled out my piece and tapped the window."

"Would you use it?"

"Hell, yes. You think I am going to let some Jheri curl homeboy get the drop on me? Hell, some lowlife crackhead pulls any jive with me, I'm gonna nail his monkey ass. Nail him dead. That way in court, there is one story to tell. Mine."

"That's cold, Gayton."

"Cold as ice. Three holdups in my stores in six weeks. I'm sick of it. Some lowlife messes with me, and he's history. Nothing but a stain on the sidewalk. Nail him dead. Not going to let some goddam Jewboy lawyer turn him into some kind of underprivileged saint." Noticing Win, the retail mogul winced and gripped his shoulder, "Forgive me for speaking out of school. You ain't Jewish are you?"

"German-Irish."

Nail him dead. FTJ-654. Revenge is sweet. To allow a slight on one's person to pass unavenged is weakness, not diplomacy. Win put down his Diet Coke and ordered a shot of Jameson. That did it. His Irish was up. Hooligan rage burned within. He was, after all, the great-great-grand-nephew of Frank Payton who bludgeoned two people to death in the St. Patrick's Day Riot of 1867. And there was his distant cousin, Jimmy. A former Westy, he was awaiting trial for dismembering a Prudential actuary who stiffed one of his hookers.

Go ahead, FTJ-654. Make my day.

The next morning a series of routine computer checks identified the owner of FTJ-654 as Howard J. Lang. Re-enacting classic episodes of *The Rockford Files*, Winfield made calls to credit bureaus, banks, the bar association, and a life insurance company. Variously identifying himself as an IRS investigator, a personnel director, and an alumni association fund-raiser, Winfield assembled a profile of the Jag owner. Within two hours his computer screen was full:

>   Howard J. Lang
>   1725 East Pomeroy
>   Shorewood, Wisconsin 53211
>   (414) 555-2424
>   11/8/75
>   BA, University of Wisconsin, 1997
>   JD, Marquette, 2000
>   Junior partner, Grayson, Mahan, and Rehbock
>   777 East Wisconsin Avenue
>   (414) 555-8989
>   Secretary: Nancy Klumb
>   Wife: Sarah Jane (Bergman)
>   Children: Beth, 12; Jon, 10
>   Income: $575,897.00
>   Tax Liens: None
>   Warrants: None

As Howard Lang's life filled the screen, Winfield's anger mounted. Five-hundred-and-seventy-five grand a year! That alone was worth a brick through the windshield. Using the S&L security computer, he added more details, following the electronic paper trail of Lang's life and career. Big law suits had come his way, but nothing looked dirty. Win's fantasy of unearthing Watergate scandal faded. What could be done to wreak havoc in Lang's uber-class world—without getting caught?

Picking up the phone he punched out 555-8989 and asked for Ms. Klumb.

"Howard Lang's office." Her soft professional voice unnerved him. Vivaldi played in the background.

"This is Gordon G. Raymond of IBM calling from New York. I just wish to make sure I have reached the right Howard Lang. Did Mr. Lang graduate from Marquette University?"

"Yes, he did."

"And his wife is named Sarah?"

"Yes." The secretary hesitated, becoming suspicious.

"Good. We have the right party. You see one of our board members met him an alumni dinner and very impressed. His name has come up a number of times. We are looking for a new firm to represent us in the Midwest. Our contract with our present law firm in Chicago is expiring, and we believe that your firm could give us the attention we need. Please let Mr. Lang know I called. I will be contacting him shortly. Thank you." He hung up abruptly before the secretary could respond.

Winfield giggled. No doubt Howie would wet his pants waiting for a call that would never come.

But driving home, fighting traffic, and realizing his Mustang was overdue for an oil change, Win felt deflated. Revenge would require more than a telephone prank.

A few days later, having fallen asleep over a stack of essay exams, Winfield awoke to a strident, yet vaguely familiar voice. Looking up from his desk, a red-mottled page sticking to his cheek, his eyes focused on the TV. Ms. Andrea Kaufmann was banging the arm of her director's chair on Public Access Channel 14. Braced by a pair of women in black jumpsuits holding smart phones, Andrea came to Win's aid. Her group was fighting the exploitation of womanhood and the defilement of a multi-racial working class neighborhood and catching offenders in the act. Win sat up and smiled.

Despite the pile of papers, his overdue income tax return, an impatient resume client, and an upcoming sales presentation, Winfield devoted two full evenings to his pet project. Working with the deft skill of the anonymous hands doctoring Oswald photos in Oliver Stone's *JFK*, Winfield carefully photoshopped images cut and pasted from *Car and Driver* and *Maxim*. Once satisfied with the composition and the accompanying text, he pressed PRINT and watched two hundred copies churn from his LaserJet. Printed on flame red paper, the picture looked better in black and white, convincingly cell phone blurry but still distinct.

The labeling and stamping, performed with latex gloves, took two full hours. He checked his work carefully, making sure that the flyers headed "Tell Your Patient" went to Lang's dentist, internist, and allergist, and the ones reading "Tell Your Partner" went to every attorney at Grayson, Mahan, and Rehbock.

"I think Ms. Kaufmann's point on Edward Albee is well-taken," Winfield told his class, stunning everyone in the seminar room, including Ms. Kaufmann. "It is not inappropriate to bring one's political consciousness to literature. All of us are obligated, of course, to be honest with ourselves. I think all points of view assist us to examine the play more clearly, if only by answering the questions they raise."

Winfield smiled at Ms. Kaufmann, who nodded and let a hint of a grin quiver briefly on her chapped, unpainted lips. Glancing at the clock, Winfield glowed. No doubt by now the efficient Shorewood post office had delivered fifty-two flame red mailers to every house within a three block radius of 1725 East Pomeroy. In two hours, the brokers, insurance agents, real estate entrepreneurs, and restaurant owners would arrive home and collect their mail. Sorting through circulars, bills, and mail order catalogs in search of tax refund checks and pizza coupons, they would discover a glossy flyer showing a leggy blonde leaning into the driver's window of a Jaguar with clearly visible Wisconsin plates. The bold caption—in ominous inch-high letters—explained the photo's significance:

**TELL YOUR NEIGHBOR HOWARD LANG,
OWNER OF RED JAGUAR FTJ-654,
TO STOP SOLICITING PROSTITUTES!
Womyn on Watch**

Two days later, Winfield stopped Ted in the hallway.

"I understand you want to get Leotha a car for her birthday. Something special."

"Yeah, I got a line on a '14 BMW with only fifteen thousand miles. Almost mint. I want to get her something nice, something classy to tool around in. Budget won't let me go new."

"Listen, I know a guy with a brand new Jaguar who might want to sell. I found out by accident. Well, I, uh, well I heard it from his wife—you know—so you can't mention my name. Just call him and ask. I have his number. And Ted, I think if you mention that you were in the FBI, he might give you a hell of a deal."

CHALK MEN

Spotting a parking space near the side entrance of Frederick Douglass Savings and Loan, Winfield pulled in. There wasn't time to park in the underground garage. Negotiating the narrow spiral ramp and dodging the support columns took at least two minutes, and Win was running late. The monthly English Department meeting had dragged on until eight-thirty the night before. There had been endless debates about the merits of a new anthology. The African-Americans disputed the ratio of Alice Walker-James Baldwin entries to the number of Shelby Steele-William Raspberry pieces. Hispanics and Native Americans battled over an article denouncing Columbus. The next-year-in-Havana Cubans were most vociferous. The feminists were neutral. The gays angry. Winfield pouted. They weren't going to adopt his book, so he didn't care. He stayed until the vote was taken so he could abstain out of spite.

Afterwards, he solaced himself with double Jamesons at The Black Shamrock, flirting half-heartedly with Moira whose Dublin accent and centerfold cleavage never failed to cheer him up. He began scribbling notes on a napkin. No doubt the debate he had endured was echoing through English departments across the country. It might just be possible to strike the right balance with a series of pro and con articles to get a textbook past a faculty committee. Fifty sections of freshman English with twenty students in a thousand colleges meant a million copies a year. Just ten percent of the market at five-fifty a book would mean a neat half million. After a Guinness chaser, Winfield pocketed a stack of ink-smeared napkins and stumbled home.

His temples still pounding, Win glanced at his watch. He had a finance report to drop off before his nine o'clock class. Grabbing his briefcase, he hastily inserted the red handled Club into his steering wheel and rushed to the back door. Climbing the stairs, he caught a glimpse of people gathering in front of the main entrance.

Passing the conference room, he noticed Brooks Adams peeking through the black mini-blinds to the street below.

"What is it? Accident?" Win asked.

"Take a look," Brooks answered quietly without turning around.

Winfield walked to the window. On the sidewalk a half-dozen employees had formed a tight ring around the chalk outline of a man. A splash of red suggested the victim had been shot in the head.

"Jesus! Somebody get killed?"

"Look up the street."

Cupping his hands against the glare of the morning sun, Winfield saw half a dozen figures chalked against the sidewalk. Drawn in different positions, they resembled dancing gingerbread men.

"Looks like the St. Valentine's Day Massacre."

"We're not the only ones. They're outside City Hall, the police stations, the Hyatt, US Bank, even the main building at MITI," Brooks said softly. "Lionel's been on the phone since seven-thirty. We're the only black outfit to be hit."

Winfield looked out the window again, trying to understand the significance of the bleeding chalk men. A light snow was blowing off the lake, sprinkling the red splotches with dusty flakes.

"Did you hear it on the radio?"

Winfield had been listening to *Sinatra Duets II* in the car. "No, what's going on?"

"Moses. This is his work. He's laying the dead of the community on 'appropriate doorsteps.' All the black homicide victims. It's not crack, it's not gangs, it's us. The white politicians, the banks that redline, the businesses that don't hire enough brothers, the hotel that only hires blacks to bus dishes, the hospital with only two black doctors. And we're the only black-owned outfit on his list."

"He won't let go."

"He can't. He can't let us accomplish something. We pull off Brewer's Court, and we disprove his whole philosophy, so he has to demonize us. If we succeed it has to be because we've sold out. Oreos. Damn!"

Winfield could not resist smiling. Two months before Moses had gained national attention by mailing Oreo cookies to Clarence Thomas, Tony Brown, Lisa Bonet, Montel Williams, and five thousand others. Every African-American employed by Microsoft, every black general in the Pentagon, and every woman of color on the staff of *Cosmopolitan* had received an Oreo. Sealed in plastic discs used for rare coins, the cookies arrived without comment.

Shunned by Oprah, also a recipient, Alderman Moses revealed his strategy to Touré. He, too, had been sent a cookie, something MSNBC interns evidently dismissed as a Nabisco promotion. Now Moses was mounting a new campaign, marshaling the homeless on another mass mailing. Every Republican member of Congress was being sent a miniature wooden cross and a match. Due to costs, GI Joe's in Klan sheets waving Confederate flags were restricted to the Supreme Court.

"What are we going to do?" Winfield asked.

"I don't know," Brooks said, biting his lip. "If we rub them out, we'll look guilty. Ashamed. Hell, a lot of blacks in the hotels and banks are going to be burned, too. Plus, he tagged the school board."

Winfield stroked his chin, lost in thought. As Communications Director, his job included crisis management. "Listen, Brooks, I have class until eleven. Let me think of something. I suggest we take an ad out in the community papers. Full page." He paused, then raised a finger, his whiskey-numbed mind clearing, "What about this? We steal his thunder. OK, our ad shows a chalk man on the sidewalk. In the center of the guy we list everything we've done. Loans to small businesses. People we hired. United Negro College Fund donations. The Urban League dinners you sponsored. The midnight basketball teams. The computers we donated to the House of Peace. Don't run from it. Use it. But don't even mention his name. We take over, make it our own. At the bottom of the ad, under the chalk man, in big letters, we put, 'What are you doing to help?' Something like that."

"That might work. Sketch something out and email it to me. I can get Kevin to handle the art work. We can't wait for ads, we have get it online today. Facebook. Twitter. YouTube. Something to send the bloggers."

Win glanced at his watch. "Wow! I have to run!"

Crossing the faculty parking lot, Winfield noticed a Channel 12 van double parked in front of MITI's main building. Her hair heavily lacquered against the wind, Jill Goodwin was bathed in camera lights. Chalk men, their heads and hearts splashed with red paint, lined the sidewalk. The artists had been inclusive. Small figures represented children and triangular women's room logo skirts had been chalked on female victims.

Students paused, made comments, then cautiously stepped over the outlines. As Winfield neared the building, someone called out to him.

"Dr. Payton, is this an art project or something?"

He thought about blaming it on the NEA, then demurred. "Shawna, it's a political statement."

"Oh, '*po*-litical,'" she sighed, stepping back to ponder the figures as if they were original copies of the Magna Carta.

Winfield expected the bleeding chalk men to be the subject of discussion in the English Department that morning. Two female professors were chatting with the secretary Janet when he ducked in to collect his mail. Conversation stopped. He turned, noticing all three women staring at him.

"You have a message," the secretary cooed in a breathy voice.

"Message?" Winfield asked, his heart sinking. His female colleagues were unpredictable, their reactions to single males ranging from radical feminist contempt to adulterous lust.

Janet waved a pink "While You Were Out" slip. "Shelly Bronfman called. At 8:30. She just *has* to have dinner with you tonight. She sounded urgent."

Victoria Peterson, PhD, former Panther and Moses supporter, smirked. Strange be the ways of white folks. Her officemate, head shorn to politically correct Sinead O'Connor perfection, tossed imaginary locks, "Oh," she breathed heavily, "Young, young, young man! Has anyone told you look like a Prince out of the Arabian Nights?" She broke into an earthy laugh.

119

"She's got to be almost sixty, Win," Janet snorted, "and she's had more facelifts than Joan Rivers."

"I thought Ms. Bronfman stuck to paperboys and pool men. You're a step up," Victoria said.

"Listen, make sure she takes you shopping first. Have her buy you a watch, something you can return for cash. And don't take a check. And, consider taping a few phone calls. Good insurance for when she dumps you for a Chippendale's dancer," Janet suggested.

"I'm sure it's just a business dinner."

"I wouldn't boast about being her client, Win. Unless you moonlight as a hit man."

The tone in his own office was no better. Quickly shuffling through his papers for his first class, Winfield turned to see Baldwin leering in the doorway.

"I hear you got a dinner invite."

Christ! Had he no privacy?

"Just a legal matter, Tim. You know how it is."

"Oh, yeah. I know."

While his students worked on an in-class exercise, Winfield sketched out an ad listing all the community services Frederick Douglass Savings and Loan had provided in the last two years.

Between classes, he dashed to his office to pound out his copy on the computer. He was emailing it when the phone rang.

Brooks' voice was strained. "Win, get over here as soon as you can."

"Sure, right after my noon class. What's wrong?"

"Reverend Johnson just decided to pull out of Brewer's Court. We've got to move fast. And another thing," he said, his tone lightening, "you received a message from Shelly Bronfman. Dinner at eight at the Blue Room."

God! Did she have to leave messages for him all over town? An audible moan escaped his lips. No doubt there would be a message on his voicemail at home, a message at the health club, one at his dentist's, another at his hair salon.

Glancing once more at his attachment, he hit SEND and raced to class. His students' debate over whether or not Willy Loman had Alzheimer's was so engaging that Win almost forgot about Moses, Shelly Bronfman, and the bleeding chalk men.

Brooks and Lionel Adams were studying the street below when Winfield entered the conference room. It was two in the afternoon, and already customers and passersby were stepping over the chalk men without pausing. Like New Yorkers navigating around the homeless, they skirted the chalk figures, who remained defiantly unsmudged.

"It's going to snow tonight. Six or seven inches. We'll let nature and the snow blowers take their course," Brooks decided.

"I just wish that would be the end of it," Lionel mused.

"What's this about Johnson?" Winfield asked.

"He released a statement to the press. Moses hit home. Johnson and the whole church crowd have decided to pull their money out of Brewer's Court. It's just a few hundred thousand, but it leaves us as the only major blacks in the deal. He's just whitened it up, leaving us to twist in the wind. He was on the radio at noon, saying he feels churches should build homes for the poor not the rich. Leaves us looking like a bunch of Toms."

"Shed is even worse," Lionel said. "I called the *Community Journal*. His column this week will name us. He is going to accuse us of tricking black churches into bankrolling a tax haven for the rich and the white."

Brooks tapped the mini-blind in thought, "We have got to bring in more investors. We promised community investment. We need more NWA's. And fast."

Winfield nodded. NWA's—Niggas With Assets—were the very lifeblood of Frederick Douglass Savings and Loan. "Brooks, what about Veraswami? Has he had any more luck?"

"We're having lunch tomorrow. I just called him. He's been in contact with some African investors who might be good for a few million, but it could be dicey. If we could get a mil out of them, it would make up for the church money and give us something to play up in the media. God, Win, if you were black, I'd want your pension."

"We need money," Lionel said, "but who says it's gotta be black? I mean that would be ideal, but suppose we could attract some other minority investors. Money no other black outfit could get a line on and from folks Reverend Johnson would never dare question. Diversity comes in all types, you know?" He raised an eyebrow and jutted an elbow toward Win.

Winfield swallowed.

"Win, you have a dinner date with Shelly Bronfman. The Bronfmans are some of the heaviest hitters in town. Last year they gave half a million to the symphony. Plus, her sister is married to one of the Blomberg brothers in Chicago. He's like three-fifty or better on the Fortune 500 list. Has to be worth seven or eight hundred million at least."

"I don't know," Winfield stammered, "couldn't that be risky. I mean Shed and Moses..."

"Right. If we get some Jews to invest, we can do some real healing in this town. Would make those two clowns shut up or self-destruct. They go off on some anti-Semitic rant, they show everyone what bigots *they* are. Either way, we come out on top."

"Well, yes . . ." Winfield agreed cautiously.

"Win, all we ask is that you put in a few good words for us. After all, we aren't asking for charity. We have a double A rating. The tax breaks alone would make it attractive to people in her league."

"Just whisper in her ear," Lionel smiled.

The black and gray Rolls Royce bore Winfield and Shelly Bronfman down Lake Drive. The iced surface of Lake Michigan shone brightly under the full moon. Hung snowmen and bosomy snowwomen rose over Bradford Beach, their eyes and genitals formed from beer cans and wine bottles, debris from a fraternity frolic.

Winfield turned and smiled. Dim pink lights on the bar illuminated the passenger compartment with rose tones. Zaftig Shelly Bronfman reclined, extending a plump leg encased in seamed nylon. Her white fur coat was parted to reveal her full breasts. A wire-reinforced half bra lifted them into torpedo formation. Licking her surgically-inflated lips, she smiled at Winfield.

Their first stop was the Hyatt. The Rolls drew up under the blue canopy. Winfield hoped they could duck up to the Polaris and spend the evening sipping drinks as the restaurant rotated above Milwaukee, away from friends, away from public humiliation.

The humiliation began with a doorman's unguarded smirk. Stepping from the car, Winfield stood a head shorter than his date. They strode through the sliding doors and ran into a reception. Cameras flashed. Eager reporters waved notebooks. A pair of ballerinas twirled atop grand pianos.

Oh, God.

"Mrs. Bronfman, on behalf of the ballet company, I thank you for your support." The director, a short effusive man kissed her gloved hand and guided her to an impromptu receiving line.

"I adore fund-raisers, don't you, Win?"

Winfield smiled and brushed his hair nervously. He followed Shelly, keeping a pace behind her in hopes of staying out of camera range.

From the Hyatt, they went to the Pfister for dinner. Max seated them at a prominent table. Fortunately, the Mason Street Grill seemed full of out-of-town businessmen. Winfield ordered a salad and ate slowly, tying to confine the rest of their evening to a restaurant populated by Toledo accountants and Florida developers.

"Listen, Win, I'm so excited I can't think about food. Take me to a disco. Let's go to Victor's. I haven't been there in years."

Victors! Tim Baldwin would be there. The whole eastside crowd would be there. Moira from the Black Shamrock. Friends of Barbie. His students. Anything but that.

What to do? Feign a migraine? Slip the waiter a twenty to call his cell with a fake emergency? But if he ducked out now, he'd lose the chance to plug Brewer's Court. He thought about his promise to Brooks. To the community. He thought, too, of his own dream condo. The Jacuzzi. The fireplace. The skylights. The cocktail bar on the marble dais. Something he could never afford on his own.

You know what you got to do, cowboy.

"Shelly," he said, leaning across the table, "I have some important business to discuss with you. Money matters. Important to the city, the community. Of some importance to me. But somehow. . . somehow . . ." he said taking her hand, "I can't think about that now." He squeezed her hand, the diamond rings cutting his palm. "Shelly, let's get a room and order some champagne."

"Oh, Win, I'll get Max to call the front desk. The Presidential suite. The one with the hot tub!"

In the mirrored elevator Shelly pressed against him, crushing her breasts against his cheek. "You know, Win," she cooed, "this is my high school fantasy. Did anyone ever tell you that you look like Troy Donohue?"

WISEGUYS

Brooks Adams was usually found hunched over his laptop or leaning back in his executive chair contemplating Milwaukee's modest skyline while talking to depositors. For important calls he used a gold plated French telephone, a gift from a Haitian investor. The high-ceilinged office with its thick gilt moldings and gold-framed portraits of Frederick Douglass and Booker T. Washington bespoke of power. Operating the largest black financial institution in the state, Brooks had clout. The mayor's office called frequently. Contractors in New York and Texas bidding on federal projects in the Midwest courted him to make their minority-enterprise quotas. The mantle of the ornate fireplace was lined with pictures. Brooks in robes receiving his MBA. Brooks in khaki flight suit in Kuwait. Brooks shaking hands with George Bush, smiling. Brooks shaking hands with Obama, beaming. Brooks standing between Ben Carson and Donald Trump, ordained.

This morning Brooks bent over a spread sheet, head in hands. Winfield, on his way to hammer out an investment brochure, passed his office. Peering through the doorway, he sensed trouble.

Glancing up, Brooks sighed, tapping his desk pensively. "Oh, God, Win. We have problems."

"What is it?"

"First, our insurance on the B-25 is going through the roof. A B-17 crashed in San Diego during an air show, and the carriers are getting skittish about covering old war birds. We have to get a new FAA check or lose our coverage. But that's the tip of the iceberg. Tower and Jay Kroll are in default. They won't make a payment this month. That's forty-two grand this month, fifty-five next month."

"Anything we can do?" Winfield asked.

"Foreclose and have another second-rate property on our books. You know how that will look on our balance sheets? Plus, we have an audit coming up. That building was overvalued to begin with. They had it pegged at three million. It wouldn't bring half that now. And we can't hold our rates any longer. I'm going to have to drop the CD's half a point next quarter."

"What about?" Winfield asked, tilting his head toward the window. Through the mini-blinds the white forty-two story US Bank building dominated the city like a mammoth filing cabinet carved of ice.

"They don't know yet. So far they have been cool. But let's face it, we made a lot of promises to them about fresh investor capital, and we're coming up short. Carlos is putting in fifty grand of his own money, and Bijan thinks he can get at least a hundred from one of his uncles. That half mil you squeezed out of Bronfman came just in time. But we need a few million to stay kosher. If we don't hit our targets, some other minorities are going to edge us out, and we'll be shaved down to a slice."

"What about Singh's investors?" asked Win, eager to change the subject. The words "squeeze" and "came" hit a little too close to home. "You know, the guys from Nigeria. They were talking five or ten million, maybe more."

"One million would be enough. But they're evasive. Can't pin them down. Every time I call to track them down, it's happy hour. I think Shirley Collingsworth has been whispering in their ear. They took a limo down to Chicago two days ago and spent the night. Face it, she can offer a lot more opportunities than we can. We've got Brewer's Court, but she must have five projects. They're smart enough to know about diversification."

Winfield bit his lip. Shirley Collingsworth. He had managed to vanish whenever she appeared at investor meetings. So far she still did not connect him with the Kwik Kleen fiasco.

"Veraswami is coming in this afternoon at two-thirty for a talk. I'd like you drop by. I've been putting off trying to force these boys, but we can't wait. They are not going to hang around Wisconsin much longer. If we don't get some cash out of them soon, we might as well forget it."

Brooks sighed, glancing at his desk calendar. "Almost Valentine's Day, and I don't have a date lined up. What about you?"

Winfield coughed. He had a dinner invitation from Shelly Bronfman, who breathily informed him that Sid was in New York representing Midwestern clients in a class action suit.

"Oh to be in love, Win. I could use a therapeutic lay just now. But Karen's in DC until the twentieth."

Valentine's Day. Winfield cringed, knowing that in less than seventy-two hours he would be expected to repeat his Presidential Suite performance on Shelly Bronfman's king-sized bed.

Seventy-two hours. With the end of the Cold War, Win could no longer draw upon his third grade fantasy of nuclear war indefinitely postponing a spelling quiz.

Still, there could always be a blizzard.

Returning from class, Winfield scanned the clear Easter egg blue sky for traces of clouds. Still, blizzards were known to sweep in from Lake Michigan and blanket the city in less than an hour. Bare trees leaned in the wind. A good sign. A steady blast could blow snow into hip-deep drifts. Classes would be canceled, and, more importantly, the private drive to the Bronfman estate would be impassable—provided Shelly didn't have a snowmobile.

In the conference room, Dr. Veraswami nervously shuffled a stack of note cards like a novice dealer. Brooks and Lionel sipped coffee in silence. Keisha tapped her blood-red nails on a thick pile of loan reports marked DEFAULT. Ted Kaleem distributed computerized credit checks.

"Gentlemen and lady," Veraswami said quietly, removing his gold-framed glasses, "I have to apologize. I fully expected Ben Ahmedi and John Obi to come themselves, but they had to remain in Abuja to negotiate a government contract. Instead, they sent their sons. Recent graduates. Well-educated, bright, but they are young men on their first trip to America. I'm not sure how serious they are."

"I asked Ted to investigate them," Brooks stated. "No use chasing after them if they're not serious."

"These boys look pretty solid, so far," Ted said quietly. "I made calls and checked some of Dr. Veraswami's contacts in Nigeria. They arrived at O'Hare on February 9th and are scheduled to fly out the 16th. They took two suites at the Hyatt and have run up a considerable bill. They've been hitting the strip clubs every night. Ahmedi and his pals did back to back champagne rooms at The Landing Strip and ran up a four thousand tab they put on AMEX with no question. They paid cash for the girls at Gold Diggers and

Babydolls. VIP rooms and lap dances. Been making it rain all over town. Bouncers told me they got a little wild but cooled it off with wads of fifties. Ahmedi bought a watch at Watts for six grand and paid cash; Obi dropped eight grand on jewelry at Bayshore. He put it on Visa, and again no problems."

"OK, they have credit and some play money. They're on a spree. Question is, are they going to invest?" Brooks asked. "We need big money. My whole pitch to US Bank is our ability to tap into resources not on their radar. We need a sit down with those guys and soon."

"I explained to them, explained to their fathers the importance of this project," Singh said softly. "To blend African and African American interests, to build a bridge if you will. To impress both our governments. Mutual interests," he said, locking his fingers as if in prayer. "The problem, I fear," he sighed, "is that they doubt the viability of this organization. Will major investors—white investors—place their money in a black institution? They seem to want to meet some white people. You see, despite Obama, they believe this country is very racist, that it will never let black people rise, especially in business."

Brooks cleared his throat with a deep, pained growl. "So any more bad news?"

Ted sighed, "They're champing at the bit to see the Coast. I took them to Salerno's for steaks their first night in town. They started talking about Vegas with the bartender. She told them how Old Man Salerno ran the Stardust and worked with Lefty Rosenthal. They dug the whole *Casino* angle. She pointed out all the pictures of the old man with the Rat Pack. They hung on her every word unless they just liked staring at her tits. We are going to lose them if we don't find a way of keeping them in town."

Keisha drummed her fingernails on the glass topped table. "Count me out. One afternoon of showing those horn dogs through Brewer's Court is enough. Ahmedi is halfway human, but his pals couldn't keep their hands off my boobs. I almost broke a nail. I've done my bit."

"I know," Lionel sighed guiltily. "I offered to show them the project, but they insisted they wanted you."

"Look, I don't mind dealing with Ahmedi. He's cute and shows some respect. But Tweedledum and Tweedledee are just walking hardons."

Veraswami raised his palm. "You must understand them. They are young, and sadly, their image of American women, especially black women, is based on movies and rap videos."

Brooks shuffled his papers and looked up, pursing his lips. "So, tell me, guys, what do you really think? Are we wasting our time with them? Can we pin them down and get them to invest in Brewer's Court? Five, ten million? One million even. I need to call US Bank with something solid. Something they would never get without us. We have to prove our worth."

"The problem is they call me about getting more data," Keisha said, "but with me it's always just a come-on. I checked with Carlos and Bijan. They never got a response to their phone calls or their email. I printed out my pdf. files and walked them over to the Hyatt. The concierge paged them three times and eventually sent my papers up with a room service order. I doubt they ever opened the envelopes."

Lionel leaned forward. "I spoke with them last night. This being a black organization scares them as much as it attracts them. They don't feel secure about tying up money in a black venture. They fear it will fail. They think we will be discriminated against or discredited. They are suspicious. Skittish."

"Look, if they want reassurances we can have Gwen Moss give them a call. We could set up a meeting in her Congressional office," Bijan suggested.

"But's she's black, too," Ted said. "Another black endorsement won't help. These boys want to be sure whites will invest. We need some high roller to put his chips in to reassure them," Ted said.

"So we bring them here for a meeting and have a white guy in a suit walk in, say he's from Goldman Sachs and hand Brooks a check for ten million," Carlos said.

Brooks shook his head. "That won't work. What if they invest? They've already seen our financials. They invest, they'll get our quarterlies. They'd expect to see that ten million on our books. They don't see it, they'll ask a lot of questions. And we can't issue fake paper. Not with all these audits."

"What if the Goldman Sachs guy just advises that it's a good investment?" Bijan suggested.

"Then they would wonder if it's such a great opportunity, why doesn't this big shot invest?" Keisha asked. "It's just another empty white endorsement. We can get the mayor to do that."

"Wait," Winfield suggested. "What if you had a rich white guy who *wanted* to invest but couldn't, one who was turned down, refused? What would impress them more than a black outfit that turned away white money?"

"Why would we turn down money?" Ted asked.

"Look, you said they were impressed with the Salerno story. Remember his son Frankie tried to invest in the stadium, but they would not let him? He set up a holding company under another name, and they still shut him out."

"But he moved to Colorado," Lionel reminded Winfield.

"They don't know that," Ted said, sitting forward. "We have a white guy play Frank Jr. and say he wanted to invest but we turned him down. We have the stadium articles as proof. Hell, these kids grew up watching *The Godfather* and *Goodfellas*, right? If the mob wanted in on Brewer's Court, they'd be thrilled. That's the way they were brought up, am I right, Singh?"

Dr. Veraswami spread his small, soft palms, "Let us be honest. Hollywood has given your gangsters glamour and credibility. I am afraid you may be right. They come from good families, but they are very naive and frankly very gullible."

"And the fact we turned Salerno down would show how credible we are. It would show we might be cash poor right now but not desperate. And it would make us look strong, that we would could push back against the Mafia, and the mob guys actually backed down without a fight," Winfield suggested.

That could work, if we don't overplay our hand," Carlos said. "Maybe we could set up a lunch at Cinelli's or Joey's"

"A restaurant might not impress them. Besides, what if someone walks in and says hello to us, it could blow the whole deal. Joey's too nosy. He'd catch on and start asking questions," Ted argued.

"What do we do for Frankie?" Lionel asked. "Hire an actor?"

"No," Ted said, raising a professorial finger. "Nothing so phony. We just host a business meeting. The more genuine, the better. We just need a few white guys, the right environment, the right ambiance. We could rent a limo, even rent a house. Borrow some place for a few hours. We'll impress them with these," he said, waving the credit reports. "I make some phone calls, get the names of the room service guys, the barmen, the hookers. They will certainly remember a group of Africans tipping fifties. We'll tell them we have had them under surveillance since they arrived. We'll let on we have contacts crews on the Coast. Scare them away from California and Vegas."

"I rode with those clowns," Keisha said. "I noticed they were really taken by the mansions on Lake Drive."

"Could we borrow one?" Lionel asked. "Who do we know up there?"

"What about Sandy Preston's place? That Spanish villa with a great view of the Lake?" Bijan asked. "Remember her birthday party last year?"

Keisha shook her head. "She's in Rome until the end of March. The house is being refurbished. Contractors are ripping the place apart to put in new floors. Nobody could be living there."

Ted drummed his fingers on the table. "Keisha, what about the house on Summit? The one we foreclosed on. It's not on the Lake, but it's the size of a cathedral. I know it's empty, but we could rent some furniture. We just need to decorate the entrance hall and the library. We can close off the other rooms."

"We'd need more than furniture. You'd have to bring in rugs and what about the windows? Do you know how long it would take to make drapes? Know what that would cost? And what about the utilities? We'd have to pay the gas bill to get the heat back on."

Brooks shook his head. "We don't have time. Besides, I don't want to use any place tied to us. We don't want to leave a trail. Any other ideas?"

Keisha drummed her fingernails on the table. Lionel looked pensive. Brooks rubbed in chin in thought. Bijan tapped his smartphone.

Winfield took a deep breath. "I may be able to provide a place," he said quietly. "On the fourteenth." *The fourteenth.* Win could not bring himself to say Valentine's Day. "I have access—for that day—to the Bronfman estate. They change the access codes every day. I have the numbers for that day."

No one pressed him for an explanation. Thank God!

"Will anyone else be there?" Ted asked.

"Not until after six. We'll have to out well before then."

"We only need the place for an hour, even less," Brooks said. "If the Bronfman estate won't impress them, nothing will"

Ted slammed his fist into his left palm. "That would be perfect. We chauffeur them out in a limo. I'll make the call from the hotel and pay cash. No trace."

"But who's going to be Frankie Salerno?" Lionel asked. "We already introduced them to Carlos and Shel, and it can't be any of us."

"What about Tony? The waiter at Garibaldi's? He's better than Joe Mantegna. Put him in a black shirt and a thousand-dollar suit and give him a pinkie ring." Carlos glanced around the room. "Anyone got any other ideas?"

"Tony does owe us. I kept his Benz from being repoed," Lionel added.

Brooks bit his lip. "Tony's an outsider. We'd have to tell him too much. We have to keep this close. We need another white guy, someone they never met."

Ted laid a firm, muscular hand on Winfield's shoulder, "They've never laid eyes on Win."

"But I don't look Italian." Winfield winced, fingering his blond hair for emphasis.

"Neither does Frankie Salerno. Besides, you're the only white guy we've got."

"What do I have to say?"

"Not much," Ted said. "Let the walls do the talking. The less said the better. This is more like an audience than a business meeting. We usher them in. You only have to say a few words. They leave. We can rehearse the whole thing beforehand."

"But," Winfield protested, feeling very small, "will they buy me?"

"Sure, remember Frankie Junior is just a real estate guy with tax problems. He was never made or did time. You just have to remind them who your dad was. Look, Salerno's doesn't open until four. We borrow that portrait of the old man and some of those celebrity handshake shots to give Win some cred. Now, we'll need a crew. I can get three or four white guys from the JCC. They're ex-cops, and they'd keep their mouths shut. They'll get a kick out it."

Brooks glanced at his watch. "OK, Singh, get a hold of Ahmedi tonight. Tell him Ted has set up a meeting with Frankie Salerno. Son of the big time mob guy. Major player in own. Big investor. Ted, you get your guys together. We have two days to pull it off. This will keep them in town until the fourteenth, and they leave for JFK the next day. That will be perfect."

"Frankie Salerno. Frankie Salerno," Winfield repeated, feeling like Sinatra getting into character to play Maggio. "I guess I could do it."

"Let's not forget some arm candy." Ted said. "They would expect a guy like Frankie to have a babe. She has to be white, preferably stacked."

White. Stacked. Italian-looking. *Moira!*

"Remember the Irish girl we used for the website announcing free checking?"

Ted smiled, cupping his hands. "The brunette with the melons? Oh sure, she added some welcome diversity. But can you trust her? Will she keep her mouth shut? A modeling job is one thing, but this is a little different."

"No problem." Moira had confided that she had overstayed her visa and was working off the books. Fearful of deportation, she did not report a purse snatching or bother to record the license plate of the drunk driver who sideswiped her Toyota.

"OK," Brooks nodded, "Let's sum this up. Winfield will play Frankie Salerno and bring the tits. Ted will line up the car and crew."

"I'll get the Salerno pictures," Ted promised. "Jimmy Pulido can handle it. He and the bar manager go way back. Now, Win needs a new suit—you ought to get something out of this—and we need to go over what you are going to say. I'll have Jimmy give you a call. He will be your right hand man, Win. Remember that. He will be the only one who calls you Frank. Everyone else will address you as Mr. Salerno. They will have their eyes on you all the time, so you just need to give them a nod. And don't overplay the part. The Pope don't have to prove his Catholic. Just assume the role. Jimmy was undercover, so follow his lead. What do you think, Mr. Salerno?" He paused, waiting. "*Mis-ter Sa-ler-no?*" he prompted. "Forget your name, already?"

"Damn," Win muttered. Immediately the second grade Columbus Day pageant came to mind. In those innocent days when explorers were celebrated as discoverers instead of conquerors, Winfield had been selected to play the Italian hero after Manny Goldberg's appendix ruptured. Climbing from his cardboard ship, Winfield met an Indian princess. Lifting her mother's love beads over her bangs, Joy Lipinski greeted the navigator's historic arrival. "Welcome to the shores of the New World," she said, offering the necklace. His black construction paper hat bobbling on his head, Winfield gazed into Joy's blue eyes and immediately forgot his lines.

At Venutti's Menswear Winfield chose a sharp double-breasted pinstripe, cut close to the waist. The humming tailor deftly slipped pins to mark spots for alteration.

"I can have this while you wait," he said in a soft Neapolitan accent. "Would you care to select a tie?"

Winfield lifted a light cream silk from the rack. "How would this look against a black shirt."

"Black shirt? Very tasteful. I have a gold tie pin that will make you look . . ." The rest did not have to be said.

At home, Winfield scanned his video collection, pulling *Casino, Goodfellas,* and a grainy home-taped *Godfather* off the shelf. He watched and listened, practicing the subtle nuances of De Niro and Pacino.

After grading papers, he headed to The Black Shamrock. Fortunately, the bar was nearly empty. He ordered a Jameson, sliding a twenty toward Moria and telling her to keep the change.

"What's with you?" she asked, leaning forward.

Observing her cleavage, Win bit his lip and pressed closer, "I've got a little acting job for you."

"Acting?" she asked, her eyes narrowing. "It's not that video thin' you were talkin' about?"

"No, no. More like a personal appearance. A modeling job."

"Modeling? Do I keep my clothes on this time?"

"Sure. Sure. Remember that outfit you wore at Sean's birthday party? Wear that. Should take no more than an hour, and it pays five hundred. All you have to do is sit in a chair. No lines, no posing. Just be in the room. Arm candy. In this case, chair candy."

"Chair candy?" Her black eyes narrowed into mascaraed slits. "Whut ya gettin' at?"

"It's five hundred dollars for one hour of your time. And remember," he whispered, "Say nothing till you hear more."

Tilting her head, Moira gave him a West Belfast wink.

According to historic accounts, a light snow powdered North Clark Street in Chicago on St. Valentine's Day, 1929. Eighty-seven years later, a light snow powdered Lake Drive as a Lincoln Town Car pulled off the hilly road and wound through the turns of the private drive leading to the Bronfman estate.

Adjusting his tie in the back seat, Win was tempted to sneak a drink from one of the mini-bottles rattling in his pocket. The car slowed then stopped at the decorative iron gates. The driver lowered the window and turned to Win, "The code?"

"7854," Win said, taking a deep breath.

There was an electronic beep, and the gates slid open. The driver pulled up the long drive and parked in front of the Bronfman house that rose from the snow like a Czarist wedding cake. Winfield slid out of the backseat, holding the door for Moira who bounced out, tits ajiggle. Jimmy Pulido popped the trunk and carefully lifted out the oak-framed portrait of Frank Salerno. A cluster of red heart-shaped balloons floated upward, bobbing to an abrupt stop when they reached the end of their tethers.

"What's all that for?" Win asked.

"Insurance. Ted's idea. If someone shows up and asks why we're here, we tell them we're setting up a surprise party. I got an invoice from Party Palace just in case. My sister's the assistant manager. She'll vouch for us. We'll just hide these out of the way unless we need them."

Winfield guided Moira up the steps to the entrance. Punching in a second code, he pushed open the heavy doors. The baronial marble foyer was larger than Win's entire apartment. To the left was a large study. High-ceilinged, wood paneled, marble encrusted, the room reminded Win of *Downton Abbey*.

Even the blasé Pulido was impressed, "Man, this place looks like the goddam French embassy. If this don't impress them, nothing will. First, nobody touch a thing," he warned. "We gotta make sure we put everything back the way it was." He whipped out his smartphone, took a sweeping video, then began taking close-ups of the desk and mantle. "OK, Win, Moira, get into position. I'm going to check out the kitchen and bathrooms. If one these guys asks for a glass of water or has to take a leak, we can't fumble around looking for the can."

Jimmy's men replaced a seascape over the hearth with Salerno Sr.'s portrait and arranged gold-framed Salerno-Sinatra/Salerno-Martin/Salerno-Sammy handshake shots on the mantle. Jimmy nodded at Moira, pointing to a chair. Glancing at Winfield, she took her seat, thrusting out her Hindenburg cleavage.

Winfield swallowed hard and sank into the leather wingback behind Bronfman's Mussolini-sized desk.

The ex-cops moved quickly. One slipped a bottle of Bell's Scotch from his coat pocket and placed it on the bar. Another wrestled the cloud of heart balloons into a hall closet. Jimmy pulled a roll of papers from his pocket and thrust them at Win. "Hang onto these. We can't have you sitting here empty-handed. Have to have some important business being interrupted. Otherwise it will seem too fake." He walked to window tapping his phone.

"They're pulling up to the gates. We ready?"

Frank Salerno. Mister Salerno. Mr. Salerno. Mr. Frank Salerno. Frankie Salerno. Winfield practiced his name like a mantra and crossed his legs, wishing he had used the powder room. Images of the cardboard *Santa Maria* came to mind. Joy Lipinski's open blues eyes. "Welcome to the shores of the New World." Duh!

Winfield watched the white limo slide around the bend in the drive and pull in front of the great bay of mullioned windows. A black capped driver alighted, walked around the elongated Lincoln, and opened the rear door. The three

Nigerians, dressed in matching topcoats, alighted, pausing to study the house. They craned their necks, nodding and pointing. A good sign.

So far so good. So far so good. Winfield clutched his papers and smiled at Moira. He heard the front door open. Two faux bodyguards, armed with metal detectors, took their positions in the foyer. "I've got a Mr. Am-dee," one of them said to Jimmy Pulido, deliberately mispronouncing the name, "an' two associates for Mr. Salerno."

"OK."

In the hall mirror Winfield caught a glimpse of the bodyguards frisking the guests. The Nigerians, smiling to each other, lifted their arms, opened their coats, and nodded approvingly. Evidently, they were being greeted with all the mob protocol they expected.

"OK, you guys are cool. One ting. Mr. Salerno don't let nobody smoke in his presents."

"OK, OK," Ahmedi answered, sounding like a Japanese land speculator shouting "Howdy!" to Texas ranchers.

"Mr. Salerno, you have visitors."

As the trio entered, Winfield fought his natural instinct to rise. He remained fixed in his chair. The Nigerians approached cautiously, glancing at Jimmy Pulido, who interposed himself as negotiator, handler, advisor, *consigliore*.

"Mr. Salerno, this is Mr. Ahmedi."

Winfield sighed and dismissively waved the Nigerians to sit.

"I heard about your arrival," Winfield said causally, letting his long repressed Jersey accent surface. "You are seeking investment opportunities in this country. We've had calls. What can I do for you?"

Ahmedi glanced at his friends, then leaned forward. "Mr. Salerno, let me be frank. We require independent verification on something. I've learned not to trust bankers or government officials. This money we are investing..."

"... is not your own," Winfield adlibbed. "Your fathers' money. Of course, you must be careful."

"Exactly. We need a good return, but it has to be safe."

"You are interested in Frederick Douglass Savings and Loan. Brewer's Court?"

"Yes. We want to know..."

"If it's a good investment."

"Yes."

Winfield drummed his fingers on the desk. Rising, he stood under Frank Salerno's portrait.

"I spoke with Brooks Adams. Twice. I wanted to invest ten million in Brewer's Court. But he turned me down. I was disappointed, but I understand. You see my father had certain connections here and in Las Vegas," Winfield said, wheeling his hands like a Neapolitan traffic cop, "that make certain investments difficult for me. All based, I assure you, on unfair assumptions about my father, his name, his heritage, his friends." Winfield paused, watching the Nigerians' eyes. They were glancing over his shoulder, taking in the Rat Pack pics. "I called back and offered to invest twenty million through a Canadian holding company, but Brooks Adams still declined. I was disappointed, but as I said, I understand. This project has a lot of public money involved. Government agencies. Local politicians. A lot of press coverage. My name, unfortunately, is still a barrier in this town. I have to avoid high profile projects like that. You, however, can invest. They see seem very interested in the African connection. You could benefit from the publicity."

"But we have been approached by some local officials who have warned us..."

"Father Moses and a man called Shed Harris?"

The Africans nodded.

Winfield smiled. "They are clowns. Buffoons. Trouble makers. They feed on the poor and can't let opportunity get in their way. Ignore them."

"We have been looking at other ventures in Las Vegas and California," Obi said.

Winfield smiled patiently. "I am forgetting my manners. Do you care for a drink while we talk? Perhaps you would like a Bell's Scotch? A seven and seven for Mr. Makimba? A gin and tonic for. . ."

Winfield watched their eyes open. "You see, we have friends. Their people . . ." he said, waving a hand to the window, ". . . know our people . . . We get reports." He delicately unfolded a Baby Dolls' bar napkin and held it up so Ahmedi could see it.

"Leaving your name and number to a stripper is not a wise move. A bargirl remembers someone tipping fifties. Plus the champagne rooms. Back to back. A bill from Elite Escorts for twelve hundred dollars and one from Cream City Companions for nine-fifty. I don't suppose your fathers or your government would approve of these expenses."

The Nigerians' eyes widened, and they shot nervous glances at Moira, then Jimmy.

Winfield smiled. "Now, I have no interest in using what I have learned," he said softly, deftly slipping the napkin into his pocket. "But you can assume that if we know, they know," he said waving a hand westward. "Las Vegas people would use this material to pressure you to invest. They'd skim and scam and rob you blind. If you tried to report them or sue, they would blackmail you. And your chances in an American court would not be good. It could take years and legal fees would eat up any settlement. You would be lucky to see twenty cents on the dollar. Now the people at Brewer's Court have no idea these things exist. I have not spoken to Brooks Adams about this. At least not yet. With them, you are still clean. Should the press hear about this, things might change. Do you gentlemen get my point? Take my advice and put your money where I can't. Invest in Brewer's Court. And then go home before you get into any real trouble."

Jimmy entered the room.

"Frank. It's New York again."

Winfield sighed. "Sorry, gentlemen, but I have business. I hope I have helped. I don't have to remind you not to mention our little visit. Remember, take my advice. Call Brooks Adams and then head home."

The Nigerians rose, unsure whether to shake hands. They dithered for a moment, bowed, and filed out of the room.

As soon as their limo drove off, Jimmy turned from the window. "OK, grab the Bell's. Wipe everything you touched. I'll follow and double check." Jimmy's men grabbed the pictures off the mantle, then carefully lifted the portrait of Salerno Senior from the wall, slipping into its protective sleeve.

Jimmy checked his smartphone, scrolling through his pictures and glancing up at the room. "Move the chair by desk over a few inches. Look the marks on the rug. Move the phone over just a bit. A bit closer to the lamp. Wipe the doors, hit the desk again. Make sure you don't leave prints or anything else behind. Make sure you have your keys, pens, phones, stuff like that. Everyone OK? Good, that's it. We're done!"

They raced outside, wiped down the front door, and jumped in the car. Rolling down the drive, Jimmy scanned the street for potential witnesses—joggers, dog walkers, delivery men, maids cleaning windows, neighbors fetching their mail. No one in sight! Winfield sank back and pulled two Jameson minis from his pocket, handing one to Moria.

"I just hope you boys know what you're doing," she sighed.

Winfield slipped her a crisp C note, "Remember, say nothing till you hear more."

The driver picked up speed and swept down the onramp to the expressway, heading downtown.

Just south of Capitol Drive, Jimmy pounded the dashboard. "Fuck! I forgot the balloons. We have to go back. Maybe some maid will find them."

"They can't trace them," the driver assured Jimmy.

"Oh, well, the old broad will think it was her husband's doing. And if she thanks him, no way will he cop to not knowing anything about it. Still I worry. I had to miss something like that." Jimmy punched himself. "Damn!"

"Don't worry about it," Winfield smiled. "No problem."

That evening Winfield drove through the powdery snow to the Bronfman estate. At the gate, he punched in the security code and followed the now familiar path to the entrance. Shelly stood in the lighted doorway in a full length white fur coat.

"Happy Valentine's Day. I'm only wearing a garter belt under this," she whispered hoarsely, tugging him inside.

"I have a surprise for you," Winfield whispered. "Close your eyes. This will only take a second." He walked softly to the pantry and returned with a fist full of tethers. Bloated red hearts bounced over his head like an armada of barrage balloons.

"Open your eyes."

"Oh, Win!" I knew you would make this evening special," she cried, letting her fur coat slide over her ample hips and slip to the floor.

LUCK OF THE IRISH

"Leotha wants you to call her when you get a chance. It's about school," Ted Kaleem told Win as they sat down to lunch at Twin Oaks.

"No problem. I'll call her as soon as soon I get back to the office."

"I think she wants you to make a presentation. She was putting together a list of people last night. You and Shel Wertheim among others. Heritage Week or something like that."

"By the way, how does she like the Jag?" Winfield never tired of asking about his secret victory.

"She loves it. You know, I almost didn't take that car. Thought it had to be a lemon at that price."

"I think the guy had tax problems."

"You know, he said the same thing. They always do. Back taxes and coke habits are responsible for half the deals on the market."

Back in his office at Frederick Douglass Savings and Loan, Winfield telephoned Leotha.

"Oh, Win, I'm glad you called. Did Ted talk to you? I'm in charge of lining up guest speakers for the school. Next week is St. Patrick's Day, and I wondered if you wouldn't mind coming out to talk to the children. I would like them to get beyond the shamrocks and leprechauns and learn something genuine about Ireland."

"St. Patrick's week is busy for me. Shamrock Club. The parade. But Monday or Tuesday would be good." Even though she was happily married to Ted, his friend, his very big, combat-trained friend, Winfield never passed up an opportunity to see Leotha. Even her voice, with its Eartha Kitt inflections, made his flesh stir.

"That would be wonderful. You see, we're trying to expose the children to a full range of cultural experiences. Too many of them only see things simply in terms of black and white. I want them to see how other cultures developed, how other people have been oppressed and prospered. Some of the children are from West Africa, and they feel a little inferior because they come from small countries. None of the other children have heard of Ghana or Gabon. Ireland is small, but the Irish have contributed so much culturally around the world. . . do you follow?"

"Oh, yes," he answered, encouraging her to talk more. He loved the sound of her voice.

"Well, this week I'd like you to come and say something about Ireland. The children have questions about Northern Ireland. Why do Catholics and Protestants fight each other when they get along together here, that sort of thing. We've talked about stereotypes of blacks and prejudice, and you might comment on how the Irish are depicted in movies, you know, always fighting and drinking."

"I have pictures from a trip I took two years ago."

"That would be perfect. Why don't you call me before the end of the week, and we can confirm a time. I have to check with another teacher first."

"My classes are over by noon on Monday, and Tuesday's open."

"Great. Talk to you soon!"

Winfield hung up, aroused but a bit depressed. Ethnic heritage was not a big item with the Paytons. Would the kiddies at Malcolm X Montessori want to hear about how his great-grandfather, Sean Payton, rent collector for British landlords, left Ireland in the first year of the famine for Virginia where he purchased two thousand acres and fifty slaves? Unwilling to shed blood for the Confederacy, he sold his plantation after Bull Run and moved to New Orleans, recouping his fortune after the war by operating a string of mulatto brothels. His brother Frank settled in New York and helped lead a mob during the draft riots, lynching Chinese laundrymen in Manhattan after they ran out of blacks. And that was just the legacy of the Irish half. What the Germans on his mother's side did prior to 1945 was never discussed.

On the eve of St. Patrick's Day, Winfield, as usual, wore an Irish tricolor in his lapel. A thin protest against the flood of uninterrupted green. Green shamrocks. Green hats. Green ties. Green skirts. Green "Kiss Me, I'm Irish" buttons worn by Palestinian grocers and Jamaican cab drivers. And worst of all, green beer.

Winfield arrived at Malcolm X Montessori just past one. Leotha, clad in a skin-tight silk dress, stood in the doorway. Winfield never got over her build and the way the bright red of her lips and nails contrasted to her deep ebony flesh. In heels, she was a good four inches taller than he was. Following her down the hall, Winfield remembered the day in sixth grade when walking behind Mrs. Neumann he noticed her heart-shaped buttocks and curved calves and experienced his first erection.

The third graders, well-scrubbed and obedient, sat like UN delegates in the tiered rows of the multimedia center.

"Win, I have your PowerPoint all set up. I put a map of Ireland on the easel. Just let me introduce you to the children."

Leotha walked into the brightly carpeted well of the conference center and placed her hands neatly together as if leading a prayer. "Today, children we are going to learn something about Ireland. It's a very small island in Europe, but over forty million Americans descend from its immigrants. I would like you to meet Dr. Winfield Payton who teaches at Milwaukee Industrial and Technical Institute. He is also the secretary of the Irish Society here in Milwaukee. Dr. Payton?"

Rising like a Fed Chairman announcing yet another rate cut, Winfield nodded to the rows of wide-eyed children.

"Good afternoon, I'm Dr. Winfield Payton. I teach English at MITI and am Communications Director of Frederick Douglass Savings and Loan. Our firm has some of the highest performing tax shelters available." It never hurt to plug. Even a funeral was known to produce a lead or two.

The pictures, taken during a boozy two-week tour of the Emerald Isle, were clearer than Winfield remembered. Thank God for auto focus! Having forgotten most of the trip, he sometimes had to invent explanations for the pictures he couldn't recall taking.

"This is one of the great houses of Ireland. Built by an English lord in the 1700s. Like many of the plantation houses in our own South, the land owners lived like royalty while the poor lived in small cottages, tilled the soil, and worked in shops. Oh, and this is Castle . . . uh . . . Fitzgerald," Win ad-libbed, "ancestral home of F. Scott Fitzgerald. And here are some farms. See how green the grass is? And this should be Dublin, the capital."

Looking up at the screen, Winfield panicked. He had forgotten the half-dozen shots of Fitzwilliam Square hookers he'd taken through a pub window.

"These are street scenes," he narrated calmly, quickly clicking through until he found a church. Glancing around, he observed that none of the kids had noticed anything. Raised on MTV, they obviously saw nothing unusual about black-lipped blondes standing in doorways clad in vinyl thigh-high boots, leather hot pants, and studded Wonderbras.

The question and answer session that followed did, however, have its moments.

"If the Catholics in the North don't like the way they are being treated, why don't they move south? Look at the map, it's just across the border. If people sailed to America a hundred years ago, why can't they just take a bus?"

Prick! "Well, that is a good question. But telling people to move doesn't always work. The blacks in South Africa didn't want to move to Zambia, for instance."

"Yes, but that is entirely different. Those were from different tribes and had different languages. But aren't all Irish Catholics the same and talk the same language?"

The bright-eyed boy with the Louis Farrakhan bow tie smiled, waiting for an explanation.

Wiseguy! "Yes, you are right. But the Republic of Ireland—that's the south part of Ireland—can't take care of all the people who might move in. There wouldn't be enough jobs and houses for everyone."

Leotha came to his aid. "Well, class, it's time for us go. I think we should thank Dr. Payton for telling us so much about the Irish. I think we can all learn how people have more in common with each other than we think. Maybe Dr. Payton would like to take a look at our St. Patrick's Day display?"

"Of course," Winfield agreed, following the children to their classroom. A bulletin board, draped in green crepe, was dighted with paper shamrocks, each bearing a Times Roman essay:

> THE IRISH
> The Irish live in Ireland, a tiny
> island near Englind. They live in
> stone houses and eat potatoes.
> Many famous Americans are
> Irish. John F. Kennedy was
> Irish. He was a very great
> president.

> IRELAND
> Ireland is a rocky island inhabited
> by white Northern Europeans. The climate
> varies widely. The West Coast is very
> stormy. Palm trees grow on the
> warm south coast. John F.
> Kennedy's grandfather was born
> in Ireland. He was a very
> great President.

> LAND OF POETS
> Irleand is a small, enchanted island
> known for its legends and stories.
> Small people called lepercons
> hide pots of gold under trees.
> John F. Kennedy was
> a very great
> President.

The rest of the bulletin board was adorned with maps, pictures from *National Geographic*, and stills of John

Wayne in *The Quiet Man*. Winfield shook hands with the pupils. Yeats among the school children.

"All right, it's time to go home. Next week, we have Naomi Bois. She is a poet from Gabon. That's a part of Africa where many people speak French. So we can practice our phrases. Remember what we learned?"

The children nodded, singing out "*Merci, mon ami! Bon jour! Bon soir! Bon chance!*"

A little girl stepped forward. "I know the most important phrase, Ms. Kaleem. *Je ne parle pas bien francais. Povez-vous me traduire ceci?*"

"Very good. Now let's get on our jackets and coats." Leotha shepherded the children outside where a school bus and a line of cars waited in the circular drive. When she returned, Winfield helped her collect books and switch off the computers.

"I think your presentation went very well. I'm sure the children will have a lot of questions tomorrow. Sometimes they're a little difficult with strangers. They either clam up or shout all at once. I thought your pictures were very interesting, especially those Dublin street scenes."

Winfield pretended not to hear the last remark.

"Win, I owe you a drink. At least a Perrier at Le Club."

"That would be nice."

"Let me run to the ladies' room and freshen up a bit."

Waiting in the classroom, Winfield studied a globe. Where the hell was Gabon?

Minutes passed. Leotha appeared in the doorway, walking slowly with a hand cupped over her right eye.

"Win. Can you help me?" she asked in a soft whisper.

"Something in your eye?"

"I don't know. I was putting on mascara, then all of a sudden, my eye started stinging and watering. It won't stop tearing. I can't stop crying."

Win had to step up on a chair rung to reach her eye level. "Do you wear contacts?"

"No."

"I can't see anything. Your eye is very red. Maybe something is under the lid. Pull it down a few times."

"I tried that."

"Do you have any eye drops?"

"No. I thought I had some Visine in my purse, but I can't find it."

"What about the nurse's office?"

"She's gone. I saw her car drive off."

"There's a Walgreens around the corner. I passed it on the way. I can run over and get some drops."

"Don't leave me," she said, taking his hand like a frightened second grader.

"Why don't I drive us there? Maybe the pharmacist can take a look at it."

Winfield handed Leotha a handkerchief. "Hold this over your eye. Don't put any pressure on it. Just keep your eye closed." Guiding her down the hall, he slipped his arm around her waist. She hugged him, momentarily drawing his cheek to her ample breasts.

Gazing through her bullet-proof window, the Pakistani pharmacist shook her head.

"You should have a physician examine any eye injury. Mount Sinai is up the street. Three blocks. I advise going to the emergency room. I have eye drops, of course. But I recommend seeing a physician."

"Oh, Win!" Leotha gripped his hand tighter.

"It's probably nothing, but I'm sure she's right. It pays to see a doctor. A druggist can't examine your eye and prescribe anything. It will be OK."

The waiting room at Mount Sinai emergency was as pleasant, in fact, more pleasant than the lobby of the Wyndham Hotel. Winfield sat on a French provincial love seat beside the ornamental marble fireplace and flipped through *Architectural Digest* and *Fortune*.

Business was slow. Milwaukee emergency rooms, at least during the day, seemed to be doing a leisurely trade. All the uninsured shooting and car crash victims were hauled off to County. The other thirty odd hospitals stood by with the latest and most expensive technology. Helping to drive up the cost of healthcare up to 18% of GDP, their white-coated technicians waited to aid the lacerated cyclist, the over medicated stroke patient, the reluctant suicide.

An ambulance arrived. A paramedic carried a small boy. He was followed by a furious woman in a housecoat.

"Did you have to ruin my water heater?" she snapped.

"Sorry, lady but I had to cut through the pipe. I couldn't get his hand out. A doc will have to get it out."

The boy, eyes and nostrils streaming, wailed, flailing his metal tipped right arm like Captain Hook.

Thirty minutes later Leotha returned.

"It's nothing serious," she sighed, drained with exhaustion. "I scraped a bit of my cornea with the mascara brush. Just the top layer. It happens. The doctor put some fluid on my eye and looked at with a special light. She gave me these drops and some pills. I have to take it easy for a day or two."

"That's a relief. Do you want to get your car?"

"Oh, no, I don't want to drive. Can you take me home? My sister can pick up the car later. Ted won't be back from Chicago until Friday. I need to lie down. I really feel rocky."

Very rocky. She wobbled on her high heels. Winfield took her arms, doubting his ability to stabilize her Amazonian form. "Why don't you wait here and let me pull the car up."

Sliding into Win's Mustang, Leotha placed her hand on his thigh. "I'm so glad you're with me. I go to pieces under stress. I miss an off ramp on the expressway, I panic. When one of the children fell at recess, I thought I would faint. Just a little blood, and I blank out. Thank God, our vice-principal was a paramedic. He's always there for me. I hate being so dependent." As Win shifted into reverse, her hand slid higher.

"It's nothing," Win sighed, savoring her touch.

"When we get home, please stop in for a drink. I owe you one. I normally don't drink, but sometimes . . ."

"I'm Irish, remember. You don't have to explain."

When he stopped, Leotha opened her Gucci handbag. "Can you get my keys, I can't see."

Discreetly fingering through tampon tubes, Kleenex, loose change, and red-foiled Trojans, Winfield found her keys, got out, and walked around the car to open the door and guide her up the driveway.

He unlocked the massive oak door. Leotha tapped him on the shoulder. "I have to hit our security code." She leaned over him and hesitantly punched numbers on a digital keypad with a long, red-nailed finger.

African cloths, zebra skins, and Zulu warrior shields decorated the walls of the two story living room. The mirrored bar was flanked by black velvet harem scenes.

"What would you like?" Winfield asked, instantly slipping into his grad school barman role.

"A shot of Martel. A big one, please."

Winfield made a stiff Michael Collins and water for himself. Seated beside Leotha on the sofa, he handed her the large snifter and smiled.

"Are you feeling better?"

"A little. I hope you don't think I'm a big baby. I just got a little scared. I couldn't see for a while. . ." She downed her drink and held the large glass out for another.

As Winfield poured, she rose and stretched. "I have to lie down. Let's go upstairs," she said, extending her arm for support.

Juggling their drinks, Winfield assisted her up the wide staircase.

"It's on the left, end of the hall," Leotha said, gripping his arm.

"Is there anyone you want me to call?"

"No, I'll be fine. Just stay with me a while."

The king size waterbed stood on a carpeted dais. Winfield set the drinks on a night stand and helped her sit on the edge of the bed.

"Oh, Win, hold me. I was so scared." She threw her arms around him, pulling him to the bed. Wallowing on the jello-like surface, Winfield struggled to find the edge but was pinned.

"Hold me," she whispered, kissing his mouth firmly, swirling her tongue over his lips. Her hand slipped between his thighs, stroking frantically. "Please."

Winfield struggled as she breathed heavily into his ear. "What is it? What is it? Is it because I'm black?"

"No, no. It's just that. . . Well, what about Ted?"

"He's not here. Please, I'm so scared."

She unzipped her dress, kicked off her shoes, and burst out of her bra.

"Please, Win."

As always in moments like this, anatomical fluctuations dictated Winfield's morality. Having accidentally discovered his mother's diary at fourteen, he understood that even happily married women found adulterous liaisons therapeutic during periods of stress.

Trapped in Leotha's long black limbs, Win's mind flashed with images of a panther devouring a gazelle on *Animal Planet*. Stripped of his clothes like an assault victim, Winfield was helpless. Leotha's long-nailed fingers applied the condom with the violent compassion of a nurse performing some embarrassing but medically necessary procedure, and during the next several minutes Winfield felt like a choking victim enduring the Heimlich maneuver. Clenched in her arms, Win struggled for breath as Leotha panted, grunted, cried, and moaned, raking his back with blood-red nails. Climaxing at last, she flung Winfield aside, tumbling him to the floor.

Driving down North Avenue, Win stopped at the first semi-decent bar he could find. It turned out to be a topless club. Sporting a green top hat and bow tie, a smiling black girl twirled emerald tassels from her breasts. Win gulped his Korbel and Diet Coke and left.

"Stay awhile, sugah," the girl called out.

Could it really be the Old Spice?

Win successfully avoided Ted Kaleem for a full week. But on Tuesday, on his way back to MITI, he found himself alone with Ted in the elevator.

Ted placed his large ex-Marine, ex-FBI, still black belt hand on Winfield's shoulder.

"Leotha told me what happened last week."

Win swallowed hard.

"I'm glad you were there to take her care of her. She panics so easily. Just the sight of blood makes her head spin."

Win shrugged his shoulders dismissively, "It was nothing. Nothing at all."

"You know," Ted mused, his brow wrinkling with thought, "Leotha is so accident prone. Two weeks ago she twisted her ankle playing racquetball, and Shel Wertheim had to drive her home."

POINT OF ORDER

Winfield parked next to the back door just in case he had to make a run for it. Reaching over the seat, he grabbed his heavy accountant's case, swollen with stacks of documents. Just in case. On second thought, he dropped it. Better to go in playing dumb. Win was good at that. It had worked before. Aristocratic naiveté had saved him more than once. He took a deep breath, checked his hair in the rearview mirror, then climbed out.

Although the 1950s red brick school had been transformed into a community center during the Clinton era, it still defiantly bore its original name. Joseph R. McCarthy Elementary still honored Wisconsin's great Cold Warrior with its crumbling fallout shelter and oversized flag pole. Walking through the lobby, Win noticed an alcove containing a massive bronze bust of the fallen Senator. Evidently too heavy to move, the great head remained, its bulbous Karl Malden nose poking between the coat racks parked in front of it.

Even the conference room used by the Inner City Redevelopment Commission bore McCarthy's image. Among the multicultural murals, crayoned portraits of

Malcolm X, and misshapen child-drawn maps of Africa was a photograph of the heavy-jowled black Irishman conferring with Roy Cohn with a lean and hungry Bobby Kennedy looking on. Sun-faded and dusty, the picture evoked a time when *Leave it to Beaver* third graders practiced duck and cover under their desks and swiveled hula hoops on the kickball court.

Standing in the doorway, Winfield took careful note of the picture, seeing it as an omen. The room looked forbidding. A pair of long tables, skirted in black, stood on a platform, forming a courtroom bench. The next row of tables, at floor level, were suspiciously covered in green felt. Shades of Watergate hearings. Winfield noted that the gulf between the tables was wide enough to accommodate photographers. *"Are you now or have you ever been. . . ?"* Win shivered. Beyond the tables were a hundred old-fashioned folding chairs. Add a few ceiling fans and wooden railings and you could film *Inherit the Wind.* Or possibly, he thought more glumly, *Judgment at Nuremberg.*

"What do you think?" Keisha asked, slipping behind him.

"Looks like a courtroom."

"Let's hope they're rehearsing *The Caine Mutiny.* Maybe Shed will finally go crazy and pull a Captain Queeg."

"Is he here?"

"Worse. So is Moses."

"Moses?"

"He sits on the commission. Let's hope he'll be on his best behavior with all the ministers present."

"Hope? Let's pray!"

"Maybe they're still upset about the whole sign thing. Moses might have to keep his mouth shut," Win suggested. A month before Shed Harris had petitioned the commission to donate funds to erect fifteen billboards in the inner city bearing the message STOP BLACK ON BLACK CRIME!

The signs were put up by a Hispanic contractor, which angered Moses. Within a week the signs were altered by vandals to read STOP BLACK ON BLACK CRIME! *White folks got all the money.*

"If he says one thing about my Dad or calls me a 'ho' one more time, I'll lose it," Keisha whispered. Win, you can let his insults roll off your back. He can call you a mick, and you smile. None of your friends are going to take him seriously. But when he gets in my face and calls me a bitch, I see red. He runs around telling people I drop and kneel for every white man in town, and folks start to believe it. I get obscene phone calls. There are people who won't do lunch with me anymore."

"Here's Brooks," Win said, pointing to the door.

Shaking Win's hand, Brooks nodded grimly. "You guys don't have to be here, but thanks for your support. Bijan and Carlos are parking their cars."

"What do we expect?" Winfield asked.

"Moses twisted Shed's arm to get Reverend Johnson to hold a hearing. You know, clear the air. All very respectable. Johnson pulled out the church money from Brewer's Court. He's no longer a player. The only thing they can come up with is the possibility that for six months they had fifty grand deposited and their money was misused. It's history. It's all bullshit. Shed just wants the opportunity to piss on us in public. That's why the press conference. He wants to air our dirty laundry and show off for the TV cameras. If we ignored this lynching, he'd be on the ten o'clock news waving papers and claiming we refused to cooperate. It's a win-win for him. Moses wants the Inner City Redevelopment Commission to boycott Brewer's Court and get the minorities to pull out."

"They can do that?"

"It was city land. Moses is an alderman. He can get the commission to demand we turn it into a homeless shelter to blow the whole deal. We're overextended, and he knows it. If he kills Brewer's Court, we go under. Nothing would please him more."

"Nobody downtown takes Moses seriously."

"They will if he can get Johnson to do the dirty work. You know Reverend Johnson. Mr. Marshmallow. All he is going to do is ask the questions Shed feeds him. And that could be enough. The whole thing is just a stunt to make us look bad."

Ted walked boldly through the door and surveyed the room. Studying the green covered tables, he muttered. "Should have worn my Marine greens so I could feel like Ollie North."

Brooks directed Keisha and Winfield to take seats behind the rows of tables. "Keisha, sit behind me so you can whisper and pass notes. We might need your legal opinion."

Carlos, Bijan, and Lionel took their seats. A few observers, community center members, women with kids, bored old men on walkers, and off-duty daycare workers moved to the back of the room and read the bulletin board. Someone had posted a cartoon depicting Brooks and Lionel as carpetbaggers in spats and stovepipe hats.

Looking around the old classroom, Winfield recalled his New Jersey childhood, fondly remembering sixth grade English. O. Henry and Edgar Allan Poe. "The Ransom of Red Chief" and "To Helen." Even more fondly, he recalled shapely Mrs. Neumann poised at the black board, her heart-shaped rump doing a slight wiggle as she wrote out homework assignments.

A group of AME ministers, self-importantly carrying leather portfolios, took seats behind Win. They glanced at the cartoon, then studied Brooks and Lionel, silently telegraphing their disapproval with nods and pokes.

As always, Alderman Moses was preceded by a pair of men in black jumpsuits and visored caps pulled down to their noses. They took positions beside the door as Moses entered. Stroking his graying beard, he studied the gathering and silently moved to the far end of the black-skirted table and sat. He removed his wide brimmed John Brown hat and placed it before him upside down as if planning to take up a collection.

Shed Harris ushered in two heavyset women who, avoiding Moses' greeting, sat near the door. Reverend Johnson, small and smiling, hesitantly took the center chair at the head table and shot nervous glances around the room before clearing his throat to get attention.

Aware everyone was looking at him, Johnson flustered, rose halfway, cleared his throat again, sat, then stood up hesitantly.

"I. . . . uh . . . I'd like to welcome everyone here today. We're here today to try to address some concerns the community has. I want to thank everyone for coming." He sat, put on a pair of gold wire rimmed glasses, and shuffled his papers.

"I asked Mr. Adams and . . . Mr. Adams," he said, pointing to Brooks and Lionel, "to meet with us to clear up some confusion about Brewer's Court. Our commission had been working with the city about building low-income housing on that site back in '99, and so we have a history of trying to redevelop this area. . ."

Winfield shifted in his seat. This was going to be worse than his freshman ethics class, a disaster of a course taught by an aphasic alcoholic one semester from retirement. He glanced up at the orange banner hanging above Johnson's head. HIGH STANARDS START HERE. Moses must have kept it as a trophy. The banner, shy one letter, had been accidentally hung over a black school. It was replaced within an hour, but Moses raced to the scene to snap a picture and blazon it across his website as evidence of the school board's ongoing conspiracy to denigrate W. E. B. DuBois Junior High.

"Mr. Harris and Alderman Moses, both members of this commission, have brought to my attention some articles in the press about Frederick Douglass Savings and Loan's involvement in a number of uh. . . activities. And I thought it would be most beneficial to clear the air. The failure to communicate is the curse of our community. Men and women in our community often work at cross purposes. And there is good reason for warranted suspicion of corporate intentions. We see billions of dollars spent on office towers, stadiums, convention centers, and hotels and nothing for the poor."

Reverend Johnson's sing-song syntax was labored but soothing. Winfield's eyelids grew heavy, and his body jerked when he nodded off. He should have taken a seat near the wall, he realized. Seated there, he could prop himself against the bookcase and, like many of his own students, gaze ceilingward to feign concentration and sleep.

"We in Inner City Redevelopment want to see projects that will create homes and jobs for residents, for working people. Now, uh, Mr. Adams?"

"Which Mr. Adams?" Brooks asked quietly.

Thrown off guard, Reverend Johnson cleared his throat twice and shifted his weight awkwardly. "Well, yes, of course . . . uh . . ." He glanced nervously toward Shed Harris, then mumbled, "I suppose whichever of you wishes to respond to whichever question that which. . . might come up . . . as we go along."

Shed rolled his eyes and tapped his watch. Moses sat unconcerned for the moment, fingering the brim of his upturned hat.

Reverend Johnson cleared his throat and swallowed hard. "Well, to get started then. Well, Mr. Adams . . . I mean either one . . . I understand the cheapest unit in Brewer's Court is . . . uh . . ."

"Four hundred and twenty-five thousand dollars," Brooks said calmly.

"Now, you know a single person in Milwaukee County receives only three hundred and eighty-seven dollars a month in general assistance. Minimum wage works out to less than a thousand a month take-home pay. Now I wonder how a single person could afford to live there."

"Well, it might help if he or she got a real job or started a business," Brooks said simply. "Brewer's Court was never meant to be low-income housing. Our goal, if you remember our statement to the mayor and this commission, was to bring more upper income taxpayers back to the city. The loss of tax base is, I believe, one of your concerns. White flight? I believe you and your commission have made statements to that effect since your organization was formed. We naturally thought you would approve of increasing the tax base by eighty million dollars."

"So you admit this is for white upper class people. All this effort, all this help from the mayor, all the state grants, all the tax breaks go to rich white people?" Shed Harris raised his hands in exaggerated horror.

"Upper class perhaps. But it is certainly not limited to whites. The grants and tax breaks go to investors, many of them minorities. Over half the contractors are minority owned and operated. We've created fifty jobs . . ."

"Fifty Africans laboring in the sun and snow to build mansions for the white folk. Something very familiar 'bout that, Mr. Adams," Shed pronounced.

"Fifty men and women making up to thirty-eight dollars an hour. . . ."

"Oh, yes and when they pack up their ladders and shovels, who is going to live there? Who is going to sleep under those roofs, swim in that heated pool, stroll around on their rooftop gardens of Babylon, have the cops protect their Corvettes and Caddies? Who is going to take over that neighborhood?"

"We have sold units to at least four African-Americans, several Hispanics, and a Korean . . ."

"Koh-ree-un!" Shed gasped. "Well, that's just what I want. Why? So he don't have to take the freeway to the stores where he robs black folks?"

"Well, I think there are other concerns." Reverend Johnson seemed pained by the Korean remark and began asking questions about property tax exemptions.

Winfield felt himself nodding off and bit his tongue to stay awake.

The minutes crawled.

"I have a question," Shed Harris said, sitting forward, drumming his fingers on a stack of papers. "Frederick Douglass used to pride itself in being the backbone of the black community. And it is clear that you have gotten rich off black folks paying off mortgages. You been investin' in Europe, buying up real estate in Texas and Las Vegas—but you have not made one home loan in the fourth ward this year. Not one. I need to ask *why*?"

"The answer is simple," Brooks responded, holding back his anger. "No one can make a home loan in the fourth ward. Not since the state condemned the tannery on Fifth Street and declared it a toxic site. No one can get clearance to sell a house in that ward. It's another Love Canal."

"So you admit deliberately scaling back on minority home loans? And what about these overseas investments? Why should black investors put their hard-earned dollars into your hands so you can run over to Ireland and build a golf course?" Shed cupped his hands like a concerned All-State TV pitchman.

"We live in a global economy," Brooks responded. "To survive we have to be invested worldwide, so we can secure the capital needed for local projects."

"Well, let's take a look at some of these domestic investments. You have on your website pictures of an air force bomber you purchased in Texas. Now how the hell does this help people of color in our community? Is this a wise use of our dollars? What are you going to do for the people in the 'hood—cheat us, then bomb us if don't pay? Not to mention the parties—receptions with champagne and caviar for the elites, while the people are dying on the streets. We're eating government cheese and watching our entitlements slashed while you take state money to feed a bunch of Asian investors who fly over here to fill their pockets and run back to China. And all those minority employees you claim you got building this Taj Mahal? I looked at the payroll lists. Since when is people named Goldman, Cohen, and Rubenstein minorities? How cum they getting black people's money?"

Reverend Johnson looked pained. Moses nodded in glum agreement. Folding chairs scraped, and the ministers behind Winfield muttered.

"I don't want to sound anti-Septic—but since when did a bunch of Jews hire any of us to build one of their temples? And I've come across some interesting little tactics used by Frederick Douglass Savings and Loan in selling property to unsuspecting investors. I notice time and time again, NWA written on memos we have collected."

"You went through our trash?" Lionel asked.

"How these documents were obtained is not the issue. Do you refuse to confirm that you have targeted NWA's— Niggers With Assets as you call hard-working African-Americans—to buy inner city property? Do you also refuse to confirm the use of what your notes refer to as WAWA's?

I have learned that WAWA refers to White Adults Walking Around. Is that true?"

Winfield winced. WAWA's had been his assigned contribution to Brooks' Potemkin promotions. With investors flying in from Toronto or Miami, Lionel and his gymnast boyfriend rushed to a designated ghetto intersection, taping red SOLD banners across empty storefronts and putting up collapsible COMING SOON billboards in vacant lots. Win knew a half-dozen cash-strapped adjunct instructors who habitually wore suits and ties to look hirable and could be assembled at a moment's notice. As soon as Brooks texted him from the airport, Win hustled his team into a pair of cabs and raced to meet Lionel. On cue, Win's colleagues fanned out and for five or ten minutes walked up and down the street, brandishing cell phones, and entering and exiting shattered bodegas. Gathering on street corners, they held mock conferences, waving clipboards, taking pictures, aiming pencils, and making sweeping developer gestures. Brooks would roll by in his Lexus and pause for a casual stop and chat. Signs announcing the imminent arrival of Star-bucks, Whole Foods, and Applebee's and white men in suits greeting Brooks with broad smiles and deferential nods assured his passengers that the neighborhood was slated for revival and that Brooks was a major player.

"And these WAWA's were paid a hundred dollars to walk around black neighborhoods in suits and ties to imply that some kind of Anglo-Saxon gentrification was underway?"

Untrue! Untrue! Win never paid more than fifty.

"Are these the kinds of tactics you employ? And what about that surplus army bomber? How do these investments create jobs and housing?"

"Those are discretionary investments apart from the savings and loan. Totally separate businesses. I also buy savings bonds and donate to the United Negro College

Fund, but I don't suppose that appears in your report, or does it? A fifteen thousand donation last year and twenty-thousand-dollar donation this year. You have that noted, don't you?" Brooks asked, trying to soften the edge in his voice.

"No . . . uh. . . huh. . . . I do not at this time. . . But what did you want with a bomber anyway? Was you going to sell this to . . . uh. . . . a foreign country or something?" Johnson asked.

"Reverend Johnson, the plane is an antique. It's seventy-five years old. A museum piece really. An important reminder of our veterans' sacrifice in World War II. We plan to tour the country with this plane and demonstrate our commitment to education and national defense." Brooks' neck flinched. "Besides, how I spend my money should be my business."

Shed leaned forward, "Well, there is a question here about Brewer's Court. This was supposed to help the community. Now if no one in the neighborhood can afford these luxury units, I don't see the benefit of an enterprise zone designation."

"Remember, you can't measure this project by its housing impact alone. It is going to create jobs. There will be three restaurants, shops, offices."

Shed Harris shot his hand into the air. "Just what kind of jobs are we talking 'bout here? Bussing dishes, waitin' tables, parkin' cars? Folks got those jobs now. All this will do is gentrify and whitey-fy the neighborhood and drive out the people of color. You're building a high-walled ghetto for rich white folks and their colored friends who can get in because they gots the green and drive a BMW. How does this help the community? And one mo' thing!" He tapped an investor brochure. "Check out the bottom of page four. You say, an' I quote, 'Brewer's Court offers residents the latest in electronic security.' *E*-lectronic security. Cameras and guards and sensors. Well, I wanna know just who you tryin' to keep out?"

"These residents will be consumers," Brooks interrupted, hoping to cut off Shed. "This will bring hundreds of new people to the community who will shop, drink, and dine in the area."

"Oh sure!" Shed spat. "Once these rich fays move in, oh sure, I kin see 'em racing 'cross the street to eat ribs 'n catfish at Sambo's Pool Hall and gettin' their dredlocks done at Sunny's Beauty. Shee! Sounds like Atlantic City all over again. You ever see how the Boardwalk has helped black business in that town? You ever see a white gambler leave Trump's palace where he just dropped ten grand and so much as walk three blocks to spend ten bucks for a Miller Lite and rib sanwitch? No way! This place is no different. You say you gots restaurants, bars, and dry cleaning right in Brewer's Court. You got a self-contained little gold-plated haven there. These honkies might as well be on a cruise ship sailing down Niggah River. They ain't gettin' off and spendin' dime one no place else."

"First of all," Brooks insisted, "we are not building a casino. This is a commercial and residential center. When we open, we plan to have local merchants exhibiting their wares. They're integrated into the project from the beginning. We'll have walking tours of the neighborhood, introducing residents to businesses in the area. We've given out two small business loans already for merchants to expand or rehab their operations. Let's remember, the brewery buildings have been empty for twenty-five years. How can any development, any use of vacant buildings be a detriment?"

"Yes, but the community is not involved." Reverend Johnson sat forward, seeking to regain control. "None of us have seen the plans you talk about. Who got these two business loans? Why aren't we informed?" he asked, raising empty palms to the ceiling.

"Reverend," Brooks stated firmly, "you pulled out of the project months ago. You got your investment back with interest. I don't see how you can refuse to take part in something and then complain that you are not included. You can't quit a job then complain about being unemployed can you?"

Reverend Johnson shuffled his papers. He glanced nervously about the table. The women looked troubled. Shed scowled, scribbling notes on a legal pad. Disapproving grumbles came from the back of the room.

Keisha leaned over and whispered to Winfield, "Moses has not said a word. He's just playing with his hat and looking at his watch. Something is going on. I can feel it. He never usually lets Shed take all the limelight. He's sitting there letting Johnson make a fool of himself."

Winfield sighed. So much for the anticipated drama. No Watergate smoking guns here.

Reverend Johnson droned on. "I just dunno. We have poor black people in this city. People who need homes, jobs, daycare. I hear about all kinds of billionaires gettin' tax breaks to build stadiums for baseball teams and the university building labs and the hotels adding rooms and swimming pools. When I ask how come no one builds affordable housing, no one can give me an answer. You business people can design skyboxes and saunas, how cum you can build jus' plain houses? We got a governor pushing poor women off welfare into jobs with no daycare for their childrens. Now, I do like to see smart black young men going places and starting businesses, and I like to see these ole buildings preserved and not torn down. But all I hear is that poor folk is being left behind again to mop floors and wait tables." The heavy black women flanking him were tired. Operating on automatic pilot, they nodded approval, their heavy-lidded eyes drooping.

There were coughs and mutters. An old man tapped his cane with impatience. Another clicked his dentures. Loudly. Reverend Johnson, running out of steam, droned and fumbled on. "I still have some questions about all this. . . uh . . . the community has needs.. . uh. . . and concerns. We must protect. . .uh. . .what we feel . . . are important concerns. We have to be a part. . . . of anything that affects the people. . . .and . . . I want to thank you all. . . for coming." Eager for his closing words, people clambered to their feet, stretched, and began picking up purses and briefcases. "And we will . . . uh. . . continue to address these issues. . . at our next meeting. . . which will be. . . ." Johnson rummaged through his papers, then scanned the walls worriedly looking for a calendar. He turned to the women behind him, but they were napping. "Our next meeting. . . will be. . . sometime next month. . . it's on the web page site. . . I think."

He bowed and busied himself collecting papers.

Keisha leaned toward Win, "What a fuddy duddy. You see his whole board is a joke."

"Yes, but the people in city hall respect his judgment," Win said.

"White folks love black men without balls," Keisha replied. "But I think we dodged the bullet this time."

"Thank God." Win felt the tension drain from his neck and back.

Brooks leaned over the back of his chair. "Notice how fast they beat it to the door to talk to the press. We bat down every single objection, but they still run to the press to make a statement. They waste our time, but they still get their names in the paper."

"If nothing else, Shed gets another negative article for his file. He wants a nice fat file to hand to the whi-whi's to kill our deal. If blacks won't support a black project, why should whites?"

"There could be more going on. Johnson's a clown, but these meetings give Moses a soapbox, and today he kept his mouth shut. Why? He never lets someone steal the show. Watch for another Oreo fight."

The school lobby was bathed with camera lights. Shed Harris was delivering a statement. Reverend Johnson, clutching papers to his chest like a life preserver, tried to look concerned and supportive.

"Exploitation and discrimination is always abhorrent, no matter what color it comes in. When minorities cynically use government programs to front for corporate interests and use their complexion as a smokescreen to sell out their community, it is doubly offensive. It must be exposed. It must be resisted. I have proof, evidence just come into my possession about the so-called African investors in this project. I plan to turn this over to the Justice Department for a full investigation."

Brooks stopped in his tracks. "Here it comes," he hissed over his shoulder. "He's gotta sling mud in public. We're going to have to listen to this bullshit. When he's done, the media will expect us to respond."

"Stay cool, Brooks," Lionel urged softly. "Stay cool and let Keisha do the talking. Women always looks better on TV answering charges. At least you get the female whi-whi's taking her side. It's the whole OJ thing."

"Thanks," Keisha sighed.

Brooks smiled, "Right, Keisha just be cool, smart, and kosher. Shed will come off like a loudmouth. OK, Keisha does the talking. Lionel and Win, you stand behind her. Win, I need your white Gesicht in camera view, a little Caucasian credibility will help."

Keisha tugged Winfield's arm. "Look out the window, what is Moses up to?"

Moses' bodyguards were waving frantically at a passing car, motioning a battered Buck Regal up the drive like sailors guiding a damaged Hellcat onto the deck of a pitching aircraft carrier. The obese driver stepped out and ambled toward the door.

"Who is that?" Lionel asked. "Ted, can you make him?"

"Doesn't look familiar. Win, you know the guy?"

Winfield studied the squat middle-aged white man. His thinning black hair was plastered to his skull like Jack Ruby's. Scowling, he moved his heavy body awkwardly up the steps, pulling his raincoat over his rumpled brown suit.

"He looks like Rodney Dangerfield," Lionel laughed nervously.

"He ain't Moses' brother, that's for sure. But something's up."

Moses' men paid unusual respect to the white man, clearing the crowd for him to enter.

Making his way across the lobby, the man called out names like a bored corporal at mail call. "Brooks Adams" he said in a Jack Webb monotone.

Moving forward, Brooks answered, "Yes?"

The white man deftly slapped a paper into Brooks' hand.

"Lionel Adams," the man said, pointing a paper into Lionel's face.

"Keisha Jackson."

"Brooks," she hissed, "it's a subpoena. Win, he's a process server. Beat it if he calls your name."

Camera lights flashed. Shed slipped out of range as the reporters crowded in.

"It looks like officers of Frederick Douglass Savings and Loan are being served to appear before a grand jury as I speak." A reporter flipped her hair from her Botoxed face and pressed forward. "Mr. Adams, Mr. Adams, what is your reaction? Father Moses has accused you of laundering drug money from Nigeria? Is this now the subject of an official investigation?"

"Yo! Yo!" Moses shouted. "Yo, Adams, we gots you now. Yo ass is grass. Gran jury gonna clean your clock for what you done. Gran jury gonna skin you alive, man!"

Pushing through the reporters, the sour-faced process server called out like a railroad conductor announcing a seldom-used suburban station, "Win-field Pay-ton . . . Win-field Pay-ton. . . Win-field Pay-ton."

Win froze. The squat man turned, searching the crowd of blacks for a response. "Win-field C. Pay-ton." He turned and gazed in Win's direction, looking directly over his shoulder at a Baptist minister coming out of the men's room. "Winfield C. Payton?" The pastor shook his head, and the process server brushed past Win as if he were invisible. Pausing before another minister, the owlish man repeated, "Win-field C. Pay-ton?"

Win folded a newsletter and grabbed his pen as if taking notes and melted into the pool of white reporters. As he slipped from a side door, he nearly ran into Mary Houlihan sneaking a cigarette outside her news van.

"Oh, Winfield!"

He winced, afraid the process server was in earshot.

"Winfield!"

"Yeah, yeah," he said hurriedly, waving in fast acknowledgment to shut her up.

"What are you doing here?"

"Oh, I take an interest in the community. MITI and all." Houlihan's station had crowned Father Moses as their darling representative of the oppressed. There was talk of taking his weekly half hour harangue from podcast to cable.

"Win, this is a surprise. You know I've got something to ask you. I can't believe my luck running into you. You have to confirm something for me. Off the record, of course."

177

Off the record. Winfield swallowed hard. Next to *Trust me* the phrase *off the record* was the most ominous thing anyone could ever hear.

"What is it?"

"Look," she said, slipping a *Shepherd's Express* from her shoulder bag. "I got an advance issue. I'm sure you've seen this."

"Mm?" Win glanced over her shoulder at the page. Amid the blurry nudes and phone sex ads, Art Krumb's "Beertown Blues" column was heavily circled in red.

"Art says, '. . . in between donating a cool half mil. to the ballet and dropping 50 grand at a homeless benefit (dressed in politically incorrect fur) Ms. Bronfman finds time to expand her stable of toy boys. Recent addition: last year's Irishman of the Year, Winny P.' Winny P? Come-on, that has to be you."

Trapped, caught, humiliated, besieged, Winfield sighed. Feeling like Clinton confronted with a stained dress, he looked at the reporter and muttered, "No comment."

THY NAME IS WOMAN

Like anyone toiling in academia, Winfield Payton suffered his share of boors. Over the years he had developed a grudging tolerance toward the smirkers, the know-it-alls, the under-medicated schizophrenics, the drunks, the dopers, the day-dreamers, the texters, the whiners (*"Not another paper!"*). He even welcomed the disdainful, patronizing questions put to him by undergraduate Mensa deconstructionists, radical feminists, Standard English-is-Fascism dialect preservationists, diehard what-happened-to-the-Soviet-Union-changes-nothing Marxist-Leninists, and We-Reject-All-Your-Western-Ism's-Islam-Is-The-Solution-Muslims. But he could not abide snoozers. Self-conscious exhaustion or hangovers were one thing, but students who buried their heads in their folded arms or tossed themselves back over their chairs like whiplash victims and shamelessly slept were intolerable.

Winfield's summer session of Business Communications 201 was actually interesting for once. This class included two financial advisors brushing up on their writing skills while on appeal. And there were no fewer than three thirty-something female executives from Bank One, all divorced, and, if their choice of skirts and lipstick were any indication, readily available. Then there was Jason Quirn. Tall, lean, handsome, the nineteen-year-old never failed to promptly fall asleep in class each day during the first week.

Late in the second week, Jason Quirn failed to appear, missed three assignments, and was presumed dropped. This left Winfield free to concentrate on the Bank One execs. During his lectures, he noticed the quick sidelong glances and polite smiles flashing between them and the convicted advisors. All of this was promising. Simple subtraction left one tight-skirted, lip-sticked Bank One exec unattended.

The class went on swimmingly from eleven to twelve-fifty each day. While the undergraduates rushed off to other classes or summer jobs, Winfield joined the advisors and Bank One execs for drinks. They made a perfect sextet sipping Diet Cokes in the Student Union. Three well-dressed couples amid the swirl of boys and girls in denim and leather. Having missed out on Enron and *Too Big to Fail*, the execs were infatuated with the detailed legal maneuvers the advisors were mounting to delay incarceration. Ladies love outlaws, and mutual fund bandits were as close as these suburban Republicanettes could come to Jeff Skilling and Dick Fuld. Win, himself, made a point of describing his colorful, though limited role, in the multi-million-dollar collapse of Brewer's Court. He was out a condo, his down payment, his consulting contracts, his plush office in Frederick Douglass Savings and Loan, his title of Communications Director, but if could entice one of the Bank One divorcees into a hot tub at County Galway, it just might be worth it. As yet he had not determined which one of the women to approach first. He sensed his chances would improve if he gallantly stepped aside for the condemned and take whomever was left. No doubt the prospect of a prison term put the advisors' hormones into high gear.

It was after one such afternoon in the Union that Winfield returned to his office to discover the snoozer dozing outside his door.

"Dr. Payton, can I talk to you?"

Win was in too good a mood to object, granting an undergraduate an undeserved office hour.

"Sure, come in. Have a seat."

But Jason Quirn did not sit. Eyes reddened, his large Nikes squeaking softly on the tiled floor, he wobbled uneasily and began speaking in low, mournful tones.

"Dr. Payton, I know I've missed a lot of class."

"Almost two weeks. That's equivalent to over a month during the regular semester."

Quirn nodded his curly blond head. "I know. I know. I just don't want to fail this class. It's the only thing I've got going right now." He sighed, his chest heaving.

"Well . . . ."

"You see, I'm from Appleton."

Winfield nodded, wondering if there was more to his plight than being from Houdini's home town.

"I came here with my girlfriend. We went steady all four years at East High. And we decided to go to college together, and we got this apartment on Oakland, and things went OK until this summer. I wanted to go to summer school at MITI because it's cheaper than Marquette, and she was going to work as a secretary because we needed some extra money for a flat screen. Well, back in May she used to come home every night right at five-thirty. Then two weeks later she began coming home at six and then seven. Then she started staying out till ten or eleven. She said she was going to happy hours with the girls from the office. Then in June, a couple of nights she didn't come home at all, and she told me she stayed at a friend's place because she had too many Alabama slammers and didn't want to drive drunk. Well, things just got worse."

Winfield felt a tightness growing in his chest, and he stopped rocking his swivel chair. Quirn was getting teary-eyed.

"Well, then the sex stopped. She wouldn't even let me touch her. And then I came home three weeks ago, and she was packing. Putting all her stuff in boxes, even the sweaters I bought her at Gurnee Mills. She said there were never any girls at the office. She was going with her boss the whole time. He's married, so he got her an apartment in Downer Estates, and he's buying her a car. A Camaro. And she just left. I don't even have a phone number. When I went to Downer Estates, the manager threw me out. I don't know what to do. This was the only girl I ever went out with. Since I was fourteen. I don't know. I don't have any friends here. I can't study. I don't know whether to stay in school or quit and go back to Appleton. I can't sleep, so every night I go out drinking."

The last words were choked. Win cleared his throat, his heart aching for this 6'2" block of adolescent pain. Even with his suppressed sniveling, he was cute. A boyish Paul Newman. Jeez, kid, Win thought, just stay away from The Black Cat.

"Well, I don't know what to say," Winfield began, his own heart empathetically aching with memories of LeAnn in high school, Vicki in college, Shireen in grad school, and lastly Barbie who had not returned his calls for three weeks. What was there to say? Track the bitch down, slug the bastard, call his wife, and cart the wayward bimbo back to your pad? Contact the campus ministry? Call an escort service? Blow your brains out and hope Miss Appleton is torn with Blanche DuBois guilt for the rest of her worthless life? Win's mind swam with notions and poses. He wavered between asking supportive Dr. Phil questions and coming on strong with some retro Rat Pack wisdom—*listen, pal, wait till you're my age. Every three or four years some broad is going to put your heart in a blender. Find 'em and forget 'em!*

"Well," Winfield found himself saying, "you have to get a grip on yourself. Getting drunk every night never solved anything." Win had a four-hundred-dollar bar tab at The Black Shamrock to attest to that. "You have to concentrate on something meaningful, something to give your life purpose. And there is nothing like an introductory business communications course to provide just that. Now, if you don't want to drop out, you'll need to catch up. Write some collection letters. Just keep busy."

"I know, but I just can't stop thinking about her and some of the things she said. She told me that this guy really turned her on. She said she never knew how good sex could be until she met him."

Winfield waved his hand dismissively. In another minute the kid would be balling out loud. "Don't believe that. She's probably scared to death of leaving you. What will her parents think? What if his wife finds out? What will her friends say? She has to run you down to convince herself she's doing the right thing. Don't take any of that stuff seriously. Why would she go out with you for four years if you were no good for her? There must have been plenty of other guys at West High."

"East."

"What?"

"East. We went to Appleton East, Dr. Payton."

"Whatever. You weren't the only guy there, right? She had chances with other boys, so why would she stick with you?"

"I know. I just needed to talk with someone. I wanted to call my Mom, but she's in Italy."

Winfield swallowed. Just the Saturday before, after leaving six messages on Barbie's voicemail and written and deleted three emails, he had called his own mother. Thankfully, she was out, and Win hung up, too drunk to leave an articulate message.

"OK, well, just follow this," Winfield said, hastily circling missed assignments on a spare syllabus like an impaired internist scribbling a prescription for Prozac. "You write a draft of a business letter and bring it to class tomorrow. We'll have a few beers . . . uh, a few Diet Cokes at the Union." He regretted the offer, wondering if the free Bank One exec might fall for Quirn. She could easily rationalize an affair with a despondent young man, telling herself she was saving him from suicide, homosexuality, or a lifetime of expensive and ineffectual psychotherapy. Anything to keep him from ending up on *Jerry Springer* in a dress.

Jason Quirn accepted the syllabus like a conscript ordered to the Russian Front.

Walking home, Win stopped at The Black Shamrock and added eighteen-seventy-five to his bar tab, leaving his last three limp dollar bills as a tip to Moira. Money was lean during the summer. His last Frederick Douglass Savings and Loan check had bounced, and no one had offered him a dime in kill fees.

In the lobby of the Downer Estates he collected his mail, scanning the boxes for fresh labels. I'd kill to know what she looks like, Winfield thought, cursing himself for not asking Quirn her name. He could easily find out but dismissed the idea. Don't get too close, a voice cautioned him. It's way too teenage.

Winfield took the elevator to the third floor, trudged down the hall, entered his flat, and went through the mail. Standing over the recycling bin, he tore up a rejection slip, shredded a pair of charity requests, carefully set aside a car wash coupon, and glumly opened bills from AMEX, MasterCard, Visa, and Discover. Dejected, he headed to the study, clicked on the remote and channel surfed while contemplating a new screenplay good enough for a kill fee. He was flashing between True TV's coverage of a copyright infringement trial and *The Great Gatsby* when he noticed the voicemail light pulsing on his telephone.

Pressing the button, he expected a call from his mother or an invitation to a last minute racquet ball game. He was feeling down enough to welcome a call from Shelly Bronfman. At first he didn't recognize the breathy voice. Then he heard the unmistakable sound of spanking, flat loving blows against willing flesh. Barbie! His heart froze. Then came more sighing. "I just want you to know. . . just want you to know I don't need you . . . I found someone better . . ." A male voice, choked with rhythmic gasps asked, "Who you calling, bitch?" Then he heard Barbie again—a chain of sighs and gasps leading to panting and woman-in-labor groans. Hearing the last of her orgasm spill from the machine, Winfield buried his face in his hands and wept.

Mark Connelly's fiction has appeared in *Indiana Review*, *Cream City Review*, *Milwaukee Magazine*, *The Ledge*, *The Great American Literary Magazine*, and *Digital Papercut*. He received an Editor's Choice Award in *Carve Magazine*'s Raymond Carver Short Story Contest in 2014; in 2015 he received Third Place in *Red Savina Review*'s Albert Camus Prize for Short Fiction. In 2005 Texas Review Press published his novella *Fifteen Minutes*, which received the Clay Reynolds Award.

Made in the USA
Monee, IL
22 December 2021